# The NO-NONSENSE GUIDE to

# RELIGION

**Symon Hill**

'Publishers have created lists of short books that
~uss the questions that your average [electoral]
'date will only ever touch if armed with a
nd a soundbite. Together [such books] hint
~ence of the grand educational tradition...
he hot headline issues are *The No-
les.* These target those topics that a
~ers care about, but that politicos
~igures and documents combine
~urnalism is far too important
~lists.'

Boyd Tonkin,
*The Independent,*
London

**About the author**
**Symon Hill** is associate director of Ekklesia, an independent thinktank that examines the role of religion in public life. He contributes regularly to the *Guardian*, *Morning Star*, *The Friend* and *Baptist Times* and is an associate tutor at the Woodbrooke Quaker Study Centre. He has written and campaigned on issues including religious liberty, the arms trade, social class and sexuality. He lives in London.

The **NO-NONSENSE GUIDE** to

# RELIGION

**Symon Hill**

The No-Nonsense Guide to Religion
Published in the UK in 2010 by New Internationalist™ Publications Ltd
55 Rectory Road
Oxford OX4 1BW, UK
**www.newint.org**
New Internationalist is a registered trade mark.

Cover image: Tim Dirven / Panos.

Series editors: Chris Brazier and Troth Wells.
Design by New Internationalist Publications Ltd.

 Printed on recycled paper by T J International, Cornwall, UK
who hold environmental accreditation ISO 14001.

British Library Cataloguing-in-Publication Data.
A catalogue record for this book is available from the British Library.

Library of Congress Cataloguing-in-Publication Data.
A catalogue for this book is available from the Library of Congress.

ISBN 978-1-906523-29-9

# Foreword

IN THIS AGE of secularism, religion gets a bad press. Open your newspapers on a typical day of the week and discover a worldview that says virtually all the wars that have ever been fought are because of religion. According to this view, faith communities are a byword for not much more than backwardness, bigotry and misogyny. The rise of fundamentalism has further linked religion to blind dogmatism and fanaticism. Yet, as Symon Hill points out, 'for every example of a link between religion and oppression, there is a link between religion and liberation'. To look at religion through a monochromatic lens is to belie history, to overlook the diversity of religions and religious experiences, and to do an injustice to one of humanity's greatest institutions.

But if we open our eyes to the true diversity, profound contributions and transcendent contents of religion, we can have a glimpse of another universe. Religion is the basis of most of our values; it is the yardstick by which virtue is defined, and is a major inspiration for charitable works and selfless service to humanity. It has shaped most of our culture; and given birth to numerous civilizations. It is a foundation for much that we regard as sublime in art and architecture, thought and philosophy, and it is a defining characteristic in the biographies of great individuals. The most open and pluralistic societies in history were the product of religion. The struggles for freedom of thought and inquiry, as well as human rights, were often led by religiously inspired individuals. In many cultures, religion provides the main motivation in the quest for social justice, poverty eradication, and universal education – and often it is the only force that stands up to naked greed and ruthless capitalism.

It is not widely recognized that implicit in the very idea of religion is the capacity to stimulate our sense of wonder. It is this faculty of wonder which generates the inquisitive, creative, imaginative, constructive character of humanity. It produces our drive to question, to know and understand, to harness and comprehend the physical world in which we exist, as well as ourselves as human beings within this physical existence. The religious consciousness and capabilities of human beings are driven by wonder at the complexity, majesty, power as well as the contradictions and perversity we find in all that exists – and what lies behind existence.

The positive aspects and benefits of religion, as Hill shows so brilliantly, cannot be ignored or written off easily. The suggestion that religion is about to disappear, that we are heading towards some sort of Godless nirvana, is both naïve and dangerous. The need for meaning is innate to us humans. We all want to live a life of significance, with some sort of content, and sense of direction. Life without meaning is boring, banal and alienating. But the quest for meaning, to be truly meaningful, has to be something more than a selfish desire for material abundance or individual spirituality. Individualism too is boring and banal. The only arena where the quest for meaning acquires fathomless depth and discipline is religion.

This why we need to rise above and go beyond the seductively simple and binary opposition between 'religion' and 'secularism' or 'reason' and 'faith', which undermines our understanding of the complex and positive role of faith in society and promotes only intolerance. The *No-Nonsense Guide to Religion* takes the debate to a higher, more rewarding and insightful level. It provides a balanced and astute account of the major religions of the world and their role in the daily lives of believers – who constitute most of the globe's inhabitants. It's an invitation for progressive politics to work hand in hand with religion to shape a better and more viable future for the whole of humanity.

*Ziauddin Sardar*
Writer and Broadcaster, London

# CONTENTS

# Introduction

It has been both challenging and enormously exciting to write a *No-Nonsense Guide to Religion*. To produce an introduction to such a vast subject in fewer than 130 pages was a daunting task, but it has been a joy as well as a privilege to explore and explain so many dimensions of such an enthralling subject.

Religion seems never to be out of the news these days and in many countries there is an impression that 'religion is back' – although of course it never really went away. As a result, there is a sense of renewed curiosity, as many people seek to understand the background behind the headlines.

My aim has therefore been to shed some light on aspects of religion which appear most frequently in the news and in discussion of major issues facing the world today. With a subject so broad, it has been necessary to make tough decisions about which issues to mention, which to explore in depth and which to leave out altogether. While I appreciate that other authors may have made different selections from my own, I trust that my book addresses at least some of the key questions about the nature of religion and its role in the world. I hope that it will point you in the right direction if you want to explore any of these issues in greater depth.

When I tell people that I'm writing a book about religion, I can never be quite sure of the reaction – especially with people I've only just met. I've been both challenged and inspired by the variety of questions I have faced in response. I've been asked about subjects as varied as terrorism, meditation, education and sexuality. There seems to be an almost infinite variety to the thoughts that can be triggered by a reference to religion.

This range of responses reveals that religion is a topic which more or less everybody has thought about to some degree. In my experience, people who emphasize that they don't know much about religion, or don't have strong views on it, have usually thought about it more than they realize – or at least about certain aspects of it. Everyone has something valid to say about religion. This is why it is such an exciting subject. It relates to so many areas of human life, culture and behavior, and to every human society – while usually aiming to go beyond the human.

While writing *The No-Nonsense Guide to Religion*, there were days when I shut myself away to work on it and spoke with hardly anyone. However, it would be a considerably weaker book if that were all I had done, for many people contributed hugely with helpful information, practical advice or enthusiastic encouragement. Nonetheless, any errors or inaccuracies are of course my own responsibility.

While there is sadly not space to mention by name everyone who has helped, particular thanks go to my editor, Chris Brazier, and his colleagues at New Internationalist, especially Troth Wells who commissioned the book. Thanks also to my expert reader, Louise Mitchell, to Ziauddin Sardar for the foreword and to my chapter readers, Philippa Newis and Emily Hunka, who faithfully gave vast amounts of their own time to reading and commenting on the chapters as I wrote them. I must also thank the Toad's Mouth café in Brockley for providing such an excellent atmosphere for writing, and my colleagues at Ekklesia and the Woodbrooke Quaker Study Centre for their patience and support when I was preoccupied with the book.

I would like to dedicate *The No-Nonsense Guide to Religion* to the memory of my father, Ted Hill, who gave me courage to think for myself and question what I am told.

*Symon Hill*
London

# 1 Talking about religion

**Talk of religion is everywhere. Turn on the television or open the newspaper and there will be stories of conflict between religions, disputes within religions and debates over the role of religion. There will be news of power, poverty and prejudice, of revival, revolution and revulsion, all with reference to religion.**

'RELIGION' IS A word that triggers strong and varied reactions. For some, it conjures up a purely negative image, as the cause of war, as an excuse for bigotry or as a crutch for the emotionally weak. For others, it is a central pillar of life, the response to a power that sustains them and the motivation for compassion. All attempts at balanced definitions throw up enormous problems.

What exactly *is* religion? In many Asian cultures, the boundaries between religion and philosophy are far less clear than in traditions deriving from Europe. Practitioners of various indigenous religions often say that their spirituality is such a natural and integrated part of their lives that there is little sense in classifying it as something separate. And what of those beliefs and practices that display many of the characteristics of religion but are clearly not intended to? Fans of football or baseball, along with the most avid followers of celebrity culture, often appear as committed and ritualistic as the most devout religious believer.

A common response to this ambiguity is to seek precise terms. Some choose to talk only of individual religions rather than religion as a whole, but this produces more problems than it solves. Writers who take this approach tend to speak in terms of 'world religions', emphasizing only popular and well-established traditions. Smaller or newer movements may be marginalized or dismissed as 'cults'. This can lead to an over-emphasis on the pronouncements of powerful figures, ignoring the diversity within religions as well as the similarities between them. When the US invaded Iraq in 2003, global demonstrations saw Christian peace campaigners marching alongside Muslims in solidarity and protest. They may well have felt that their Christianity had more in common with the Islam of their neighbors than it did with the Christianity of George W Bush, the US President much given to religious rhetoric to justify his policies. Boundaries cut across and within religious groups as well as between them.

In academic circles, scholars have sought a way through the confusion by defining religion in terms of its various aspects. The most influential of these was Ninian Smart, who outlined seven 'dimensions' of religion.[1] However, we must not lose sight of the reality that in everyday life the word 'religion' is used confidently and without clarification by both media and public. Differences over language complicate discussion of religion, but the challenges of language cannot be avoided. We should not be afraid of using a word that has several meanings.

As unsatisfying as this can be, we are obliged to deal in approximations and starting-points. The most obvious starting-point is that religion is a human activity. However, unlike many activities, it generally seeks to point to something that is beyond the human. It operates in various types of communities. To consider one of these elements without the others is to miss out on a rounded understanding of religion.

## Culture
Religion is something that people do. In this sense at least, it is strongly related to culture. There is a powerful two-way influence between culture and religion. The form that religion takes is usually closely related to the culture and context in which it exists.

## Talking about religion

A visit to a synagogue in Los Angeles is likely to be a different experience from a visit to a synagogue in Rabat, although of course there will be similarities.

In a comparable way, religion is influenced by its political context. In medieval Europe, Christians often explained the lordship of Christ in terms of feudalism, with Christ above the kings and lords whom he had set over the people. In contrast, the liberation theologians of Latin America see Christ as a liberator, standing alongside them in their struggle against poverty and oppression.

Just as culture influences religion, it influences attacks on religion. One of the most well-known critics of religion was Sigmund Freud, who argued that it involves the creation of a perfect father-figure in God. People create such a figure, he argued, to make up for deficiencies in their own fathers. Freud's analysis shows his immersion in European culture. He was familiar with Christianity and Judaism, which involve a God often presented as a father, but he tended to ignore other religions in which this is not the case.[2]

Culture and politics are of course extremely complex and their relationship with religion even more so. No society has only a single culture, but in every society certain cultural norms are dominant. Changing cultural trends may both influence religion and be influenced by it. For example, the renewed popularity of rationalistic Greek philosophy at the end of the first millennium led to the growth of influential rationalistic movements within Islam and Judaism. On most occasions when rationalism has become popular in religion, a backlash against it has sooner or later led to a renewed interest in mysticism or spiritual experience.

Such a backlash can be an example of the *inverse* influence that culture and politics can have on religion. That is to say, religious groups can arise out of rebellion against existing cultural and political situations. British imperialism in India led to a renewed interest in Hindu, Muslim and Sikh identity, as people emphasized their differences with their Christian rulers. In the West today, several religious groups promote their opposition to commercialism, defining themselves against what they see as the dominant cultural and economic norms around them.

Indeed, a glance at the origins of particular religions shows that many were clearly counter-cultural in their earliest days – sometimes radically so. This is not surprising; almost by definition, a 'new religion' is going against dominant perceptions. Of course, it may well be influenced by subtle cultural changes which assist its growth. Nonetheless, it is worth remembering that most religions were founded by people who initially had little cultural or political influence, however powerful their religions later became.

## Transcendence
While religion is a human activity, it generally seeks to point to a higher reality that goes beyond the human. This may take the form of God, gods, Nirvana, the spirit world, the ground of existence, natural law,

---

### Dimensions of religion
Ninian Smart (1927-2001) had a huge impact on the academic study of religion. He identified seven 'dimensions' by which religion may be recognized.
- Practical/ ritual
- Experiential/ emotional
- Narrative/ mythic
- Doctrinal/ philosophical
- Ethical/ legal
- Social/ institutional
- Material

This model, and similar systems developed by other scholars, can be very helpful. At the same time, 'religion' is spoken of in a wide variety of ways and no single definition can ever be entirely sufficient. ∎

Ninian Smart, *The World's Religions* (Cambridge University Press, 1998)

ultimate reality, a combination of these or a concept different from them all. The terms 'transcendence' or 'the sacred' are sometimes used as umbrella descriptions for these concepts. Those academics who insist on studying religion *solely* as a human activity are missing a crucial part of the picture. As the scholar Martin Forward puts it, to discuss religion without considering transcendence is 'like trying to understand cricket as though it is not a sport'.[3]

Does this mean religion is about truth? Questions of truth are often a vital part of religion, although the word 'truth' opens the way to a potential minefield of misunderstandings. At one extreme are those exclusivists who believe that only their own religion can be in any sense true and all others must therefore be untrue in their entirety. For many people, however, truth is something to be explored, experienced or lived out rather than simply believed. Several scholars argue that the equation of religion with belief derives from a Western cultural mindset. Even when we look at religious groups that emphasize belief, their beliefs are not necessarily about facts that can be proved or disproved. One religious group may believe that war is never acceptable while another may argue that there are certain situations in which it is permitted. They may both put forward persuasive arguments. What neither of them can do is to conduct a scientific experiment to demonstrate that they are right.

This is not to say that neither group *can* be right. A question of truth may well be involved, but truth is not confined to provable facts. In the West today, we tend to use the words 'truth' and 'fact' almost interchangeably. The alternative is an appreciation of non-factual truth, which is not a modern trick but a return to a deeper and more sophisticated understanding of reality that has characterized most societies until recent times and continues to be important in many parts of the world.

This can include mythical truth, in which a story points to a higher meaning than can be found in a literal reading. It can also involve the truth of experience, which is a starting point for many religions. Muhammad began reciting the Qur'an because he experienced a revelation in which he was given the words, not because he engaged in a purely rational process to decide what was true. Likewise, Jesus' disciples experienced his resurrection. It was not until later that they sought to explain what this experience meant.

The notion of experiential truth clearly throws up its own problems, which we shall explore in Chapter 3. However, this emphasis on experience is very appealing to many people today as it sits easily with current cultural trends that focus on the individual.

This cultural emphasis has popularized the idea of a personal spiritual journey in which an individual can engage, learning from various traditions and methods along the way. This is not a new idea; the notion of a religious journey has a long pedigree. The Buddha encouraged his disciples to 'believe nothing on the sole authority of your masters... believe what you yourself have tested'.[4] The 13th-century Jewish writer Abraham Abulafia spoke of a mystical journey into the mind that modern writers have compared to psychotherapy.[5]

But personal quests for meaning do not in themselves make religions. A religion differs from a purely individual spirituality in the vital element of community, whether this is a community of people seeking meaning together or a group whose members are sure they have already found it.

## Community

Commitment to a community may vary from a vague desire to worship with the same people once a week to a willingness to be martyred. A religious community may be local, perhaps consisting of the people who attend the same temple. It may be global, as with the Muslim concept of the Umma, the worldwide community of Muslims. It may include all members of society, such as in much of medieval Europe, where everyone was expected to belong to the Christian Church. Or it may comprise scattered individuals around the world, as with certain monastic communities. A person may belong to several distinct or overlapping religious communities at once.

The issues of community and belonging mean that religion is often a key factor in defining the identity of a person or group. A person may name his/her religion as a way of showing either commonality or difference with the rest of his/her country, community or family. For many people, a religious identity will have implications in terms of social standing and political power and there may be clear advantages in choosing one identity over another. In the Soviet Union, for example, the authorities were suspicious of religious affiliation and people seeking political advancement were likely to choose a public allegiance to atheism.

The issue of choice is complex. Many people have grown up in a particular religion and most choose to stay in it out of either habit or conviction. In many societies, they risk persecution or stigma if they try to leave it. However, the globalization of communication has made more people aware of the religious options in the world. In many places, this has led to an increase in religious conversions, with more people than ever before belonging to a different religious community from their parents.

In the light of this fluidity, it would be naive to see religion as nothing more than a two-dimensional reflection of the society in which it exists. While the culture in which a person grows up will undoubtedly have a huge influence on his or her religion, it would be inaccurate to suggest that he or she has no choice in the matter at all.

Such perceptions underestimate the complexity of religion, as something that relates to so many spheres of human activity but goes beyond them. In the light of such complexity, to ask simply whether religion is 'good' or 'bad' is to miss the point. Religion serves as a reason for war and peace, love and hatred, dialogue and narrow-mindedness. Religion can be used for many purposes, just as science can be used to develop life-saving vaccines or to build sophisticated weaponry. We may as well ask whether science is a good or bad thing, or cookery, poetry or politics. The 'goodness' or 'badness' of religion depends on the ways in which it is used, applied and lived out. It is to these practicalities that we now turn.

1 Ninian Smart, *The World's Religions* (Cambridge University Press, 1998). 2 Sigmund Freud, *Totem and Taboo* (Penguin, 1919). 3 Martin Forward, *Religion* (Oneworld Publications, 2001). 4 Cited by Karen Armstrong, *Buddha* (Penguin, 2004). 5 Karen Armstrong, *A History of God* (Vintage, 1993).

# 2 A religious world

**It is a daunting task to give an overview of the forms religion takes in the world. Varied over time and space, sometimes overlapping with each other and often encompassing a range of approaches amongst their own adherents, religions cannot easily be summarized.**

EVIDENCE FROM ARCHEOLOGY suggests that religion has been a central feature of human life for at least 30,000 years. Religion appears in virtually every human society, so it is vital to remember that we cannot discuss religion without generalizing, as we begin a whistlestop tour through the world's largest religious groupings.

### Abrahamic and related religions

The Abrahamic group includes some of the world's largest religions as well as several smaller ones. They are characterized by their monotheism, believing strongly in a single God (although there are also several monotheistic faiths that are not Abrahamic). Abrahamic faiths are sometimes described as 'narrative' religions, because they tend to emphasize stories and histories that explain their origins or convey their convictions. Unlike religions that see history as cyclical, an Abrahamic worldview regards it as linear. Written scriptures are very important in most Abrahamic religions and many have a special regard to particular historical individuals. These faiths trace their roots to Abraham, a Middle Eastern figure thought to have lived in the early second millennium BCE.

*Judaism* is the oldest religion in this group. Jews trace their ancestry to Abraham and later to Moses, said to have led the Israelites (or Jews) out of slavery in Egypt in around the 13th century BCE. Jews are described as

God's 'chosen people', but they have always differed in their interpretation of this idea.

The central authority in Judaism is the Torah, or Law. The Torah includes 613 laws, ranging from basic principles such as 'you shall not kill' to precise regulations about what may and may not be eaten. Jews vary in how literally they interpret and apply the Torah, which forms part of the Hebrew Bible. Also important is the Talmud, which consists of early commentary on the Law.

Jews tend to emphasize practice more strongly than belief; some describe it as a 'doing' religion. At the centre of Jewish ritual is the Sabbath, running from sunset on Friday until sunset on Saturday, a time during which Jews rest from work. Historically, this principle has been important in preventing exploitation of workers. The Jewish calendar includes a range of festivals as well as days of fasting. The home and family are traditionally the focus, although in some areas more activity takes place around synagogues. Rabbis provide spiritual guidance and pastoral care.

Most Jews left Palestine after the first century CE, and the Jewish diaspora spread throughout the world. For much of European history, Jews were the only explicitly non-Christian group in many Christian countries, and thus faced severe persecution from regimes looking for scapegoats. Not until the 19th century was there a serious movement for Jews to return to Palestine, and most Jews did not support this until the middle of the 20th century. About a third of the world's 15 million Jews live in Israel, about another third in North America and the rest throughout the world.

*Christianity* is based around the figure of Jesus of Nazareth (c.4 BCE–c.30 CE), known as Christ (which means Messiah or Anointed One). Jesus' existence is accepted almost universally by historians and other scholars, although the nature and content of his life are hotly disputed. He came from Galilee in the Middle East, taught values of compassion and social inclusiveness, is said to have performed healings and miracles, protested against the misuse of the Jerusalem temple and was crucified by the Roman authorities then governing Palestine. After Jesus' death, his disciples experienced his resurrection.

Jesus' first followers still saw themselves as Jews, but the faith soon spread into Europe, southwest Asia and north Africa, and Christians came to believe that they were not required to follow the Jewish Law. Most Christians believe that Jesus' death had cosmic significance, making it possible for human beings to be saved from sin. They vary in how they understand this idea. While the majority of Christians believe that Jesus rose bodily from the grave, others interpret the resurrection as basically a spiritual or experiential event.

Christianity is generally seen as the world's largest religion, with about two billion adherents. The word 'Church' is used to describe the whole community of Christian believers. Somewhat confusingly, it is also used to mean a local group of Christians meeting together or the building in which they meet. Some branches of Christianity also use the word to mean their own branch. There is a variety of different Christian groups but most fit broadly into the three categories of Orthodox, Catholic and Protestant. While many Christian groups are very hierarchical, others are more egalitarian and they vary considerably in the level of openness or equality they offer to female or gay members.

Nearly all Christians regard Jesus as divine and the phrase 'Son of God' is often used. The largest branches of Christianity all officially view Jesus as literally God. They use the concept of 'trinity' to describe how God can be simultaneously Father,

Son and Holy Spirit. However, many people find this doctrine confusing and it is debatable whether most Christians 'on the ground' think of the divine primarily in this way. Several smaller Christian groups reject the doctrine of the trinity outright and see Jesus as a great teacher or someone in whom God's power was especially present.

The Christian Bible brings together the Hebrew Bible (which Christians call the Old Testament) with a collection of early writings about Jesus and the first Christians, known as the New Testament. For some Christians (mostly Protestants), the Bible is their supreme authority, while others place greater emphasis on the teachings of Church Councils and leaders. Many Christians emphasize the sacraments, meaning rites performed by the Church and focused on Christ, which are believed to have been instituted by God.

Christian faith has inspired a diversity of political views. Even within the last century, it has been used to justify far-right dictatorships, such as those of Franco in Spain and Pinochet in Chile. It has also inspired armed revolutionary movements in Latin America and left-wing pacifism in Europe and India. In its very early years Christianity was socially radical and predominantly pacifist. Over time, its radicalism softened and in the fourth century it was 'domesticated' when the Roman Empire officially adopted Christianity as the imperial religion. Over subsequent centuries, marginal groups both within and outside the main branches of Christianity sought a return to this early radicalism.

*Islam* is the world's second largest religion, with about 1.3 billion adherents. The word derives from the Arabic word for peaceful acceptance and submission. Muslims refer to God as Allah (literally, Arabic for 'The God').

The starting-point for authority is the Qur'an,

a scripture believed to have been revealed by God to the Prophet Muhammad (c.570–c.632), whose preaching of Islam in the area around Mecca attracted persecution from Pagan authorities. As a result, Muhammad and his followers left Mecca in 622 and founded a Muslim government in Medina.

Muslims regard Muhammad as the 'Seal of the Prophets', the last in a long line of prophets sent to every society. Prophets mentioned in the Qur'an include Abraham, Moses and Jesus. Muslims have therefore traditionally seen Jews and Christians as 'People of the Book' who have responded to earlier revelations from Allah. When Islam spread to India from the eighth century, several Muslim teachers regarded the great Hindu sages of the past as prophets sent to the Indian people.

As God's sovereignty is very important in Islam, Muslims emphasize the need for all parts of human life to be governed by God. They generally believe that each individual will be held accountable for his/her deeds at the Day of Judgment, resulting in eternity in either paradise or hell.

There are five 'pillars' to Muslim life. First, *shahadah*, the sincere declaration that 'there is no God but Allah and Muhammad is his Prophet'; second, prayer five times per day; third, *zakat*, meaning donations to people in poverty and need; fourth, fasting during the month of Ramadan; and fifth, *hajj*, or pilgrimage to Mecca, which each Muslim should make at least once in life if able to do so.

The main division within Islam is between Sunni and Shi'a Muslims, who differ on issues including the location of authority within the Muslim community. There are many different tendencies within both these groups. For example, Sufis practice a mystical approach to faith and Wahhabis believe in a 'return' to strict practices they regard as basic to Islam.

Islam is sometimes associated with sharia law,

formulated in Muslim societies around the end of the first millennium. The introduction of sharia law is often backed by conservative Muslims. For the most extreme this means the use of certain harsh punishments with no regard to their original context. Other Muslims have a more sophisticated interpretation of sharia, while a small number reject it as contrary to the Qur'an.

Today, most countries with Muslim majorities are ruled by undemocratic regimes, sometimes justifying oppression in the name of Islam. However, they all face criticism from other Muslims for doing so. In many countries, Muslims experience persecution or at least stigma. This situation is exacerbated by the tendency of both Islamic fundamentalists and right-wing Western politicians to define the world in terms of an epic battle between Islam and the West.

*Baha'ism* is smaller than the three biggest Abrahamic religions, having around six million adherents, although they are spread throughout the world. Baha'is emphasize both the oneness of God and the unity of humanity. This involves a commitment to human equality, including gender equality. They also believe in the unity of all faiths, suggesting that they are all pointing towards God.

As God is regarded as ultimately unknowable, he is seen to have manifested himself through prophets and religious founders such as Abraham, the Buddha, Jesus and Muhammad. For Baha'is, the last prophet was Baha'u'llah (1819-72), a Persian who had originally been a Shi'a Muslim and who taught that humanity would eventually be reunited. He criticized prejudice and, in the context of his time, was remarkably progressive in terms of women's rights.

Baha'is emphasize care for the body and moderate living; this involves rejection of alcohol and unprescribed drugs. The Baha'i calendar includes an annual 19-day fast to focus on God. Social action is regarded as part of a worshipful life and Baha'is look forward to a future world government. However, they also encourage obedience to existing governments and generally oppose law-breaking.

*Rastafari* drew on a number of Jewish and Christian themes as it developed in the early 20th century. Rastafarians look to Africa as a promised land to which the black people of the world will return in a new age of peace. They regard Haile Selassie, who became emperor of Ethiopia in 1930 and died in 1975, as divine and as Jesus Christ returned.

Rastafarians owe much to the thought of the Jamaican thinker Marcus Garvey (1887-1940) and the black liberation movements of his time. They emphasize the Christian Bible and its prophecies, although they generally believe that truth can be found ultimately only by turning within. Biblical authority must submit to the authority of the 'self', aided by meditation and communal 'reasoning'. Rastafarians observe strict dietary laws and emphasize healthy, ethical living.

While Rastafari is particularly strong in Jamaica, it has spread throughout the world and now has about one million adherents.

There are several other Abrahamic religions, most much smaller than those mentioned here. There are also groups on the fringes of the large Abrahamic religions.

*Zoroastrianism* is not Abrahamic, but has exercised huge influence on Abrahamic religions and resembles them in several ways. It is one of the world's oldest religions. Zoroastrians are strongly monotheistic, emphasizing unity with God, who is known as Ahura Mazda (Lord Wisdom). They trace their faith back to Persian prophet and priest Zarathustra, often referred to as Zoroaster (the Greek form of his name). He is thought to have lived in the late second millennium BCE. *Ganthas* (hymns) attributed to him form part of the Avesta, a collection of Zoroastrian holy texts.

Zoroaster saw the world as the location of a struggle between Ahura Mazda on the one hand and evil forces on the other, guided by Angra Mainyu (evil spirit). Zoroastrians emphasize free will, and the ability of each man and woman to choose to work alongside Ahura Mazda or against him. At death each person's soul will be sent to live with the side he/she has chosen. However, the evil forces will eventually be defeated and resurrected bodies will be reunited with their souls and with Ahura Mazda.

Ahura Mazda is believed to have created both the spiritual and material worlds and the elements of his creation (such as fire, water, plants and animals) are held worthy of respect. Material things are therefore seen as a divine gift, which people are able to enjoy. Wealth accumulated honestly is something to be celebrated, but must be used charitably.

Zoroastrian temples contain fires, which priests work to keep burning continuously. Ahura Mazda is thought in some sense to be present in the fire. Although all Zoroastrian priests are male, a feature of the religion has been its belief in other ways in the spiritual equality of men and women.

From the sixth century BCE to the sixth century CE, Zoroastrianism dominated the Persian Empire, stretching at times from the Indian subcontinent to the edge of Egypt. There are now roughly 200,000 Zoroastrians in the world, the majority in India and Iran, with others in Canada, Pakistan and elsewhere. The extent of Zoroastrian influence on other faiths should not be underestimated.

### Religions deriving from South Asia

Religions with origins in the Indian subcontinent have spread around the globe. Traditions that can be traced back to the second millennium BCE developed into the range of expressions now called Hinduism, as well as many others. These faiths are very diverse, with widely varying attitudes towards the divine. They tend to regard individuals as passing through many lives in a process of reincarnation from which they may hope for release.

*Hinduism* developed in India over thousands of years. Describing Hinduism is especially difficult given the extreme variety within it. Some argue that the word itself is a Western attempt at artificial combination of a huge range of traditions.

Hindus often describe their faith, religion or even culture as the *sanatana dharma*, the eternal truth or

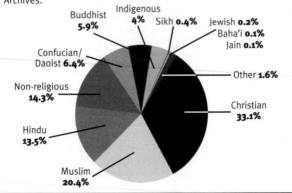

### Religion by numbers

Religious statistics are controversial. The blurring of religious boundaries makes it impossible to count adherents precisely. Furthermore, there are always people who have an interest in exaggerating or understating the size of particular religions. Statistics given here, which relate to 2005, should therefore be treated with caution and regarded as very approximate. ■

Based on information supplied by the Association of Religious Data Archives.

Buddhist **5.9%**
Indigenous **4%**
Sikh **0.4%**
Jewish **0.2%**
Baha'i **0.1%**
Jain **0.1%**
Confucian/Daoist **6.4%**
Non-religious **14.3%**
Other **1.6%**
Hindu **13.5%**
Christian **33.1%**
Muslim **20.4%**

eternal tradition. This poses a challenge to those who see religion as primarily concerned with belief. In Hinduism, lifestyle and ritual usually take precedence over doctrine. Hinduism's diversity can be confusing for someone hoping to find clearly definable branches. Different tendencies overlap and at times blur into each other.

While Hindus draw on a vast array of scriptures, they generally ascribe a central role to the Vedas, the earliest of which is dated by scholars to about 1200 BCE. They are most commonly heard at rituals and festivals, in contrast to the great Hindu epics, the *Mahabharata* and the *Ramayana*, which are hugely popular and very familiar to most Hindus (and many non-Hindu Indians). The former includes the *Bhagavad Gita* (or *Song of the Lord*) by far the most well-known Hindu scripture.

The term *samsara* describes the cycle of birth and rebirth through which individuals travel from life to life. A common goal is *moksha*, meaning release from this cycle. Hindus vary considerably in how they hope to achieve this. The most devout Hindus often choose a guru, who guides them in a disciplined spiritual process. Some rely on the grace of a god or goddess to whom they are particularly devoted. Many see all deities as manifestations of a single God, or of an impersonal reality, known as Brahman. The influential Hindu teacher Shankara (788-820) taught that Brahman is identical with each person's true self and is present in all things. Other Hindu teachers have disagreed, distinguishing Brahman from the self.

While Hinduism is vocally espoused by right-wing Indian nationalists, it has also inspired movements for social justice, including nonviolent struggles for India's independence from the British Empire. Hinduism has controversially been associated with the caste system, which divides society into four classes, as well as a fifth group of those outside the system all together.

## A religious world

The notion of caste has been used to suggest divine sanction for social inequality. However, many regard caste as a generally Indian, rather than specifically Hindu, notion and a number of Hindu teachers reject caste all together. Similarly, patriarchal practices such as *sati* – by which a widow burns to death on her husband's funeral pyre – have been strongly opposed by Hindu feminists, although they still have their defenders.

There are about 900 million Hindus, making Hinduism the world's third largest religion.

*Jainism* is related to Hinduism, having developed out of Indian ascetic traditions in the first millennium BCE. Jains seek detachment from material existence in order to be freed from karma and rebirth. They are known particularly for their strong commitment to *ahimsa* (nonviolence).

Jains trace their tradition back to Parsvanatha, thought to have lived in the ninth century BCE. However, the religion owes much to Mahavira Vardhamana, known as the Jina (or victor), who lived about three centuries later. By his time, Jains were committing themselves to the five vows of *ahimsa*, truthfulness, refusal to steal, sexual restraint and non-possession.

Jains go to great lengths to avoid harm to any creature. Jain monks and nuns not only live a vegan lifestyle, but will sweep the path in front of them so as to cause no harm to insects. They choose forms of cleanliness that avoid harm to minute water-borne life. While lay Jains are not required to live up to this monastic standard, high levels of nonviolence are expected, including in the employment they are willing to take up.

While some have seen Jain attitudes as a withdrawal from the world, Jains have often been led by their commitments to show care for both humans and animals who are experiencing violence. Some Jains, such as Acarya Tulsi (1914-97) have actively promoted nonviolence at a political level.

There are slightly more than four million Jains alive today, the majority in India.

*Buddhism* developed in India slightly later, about 2,500 years ago. Buddhists emphasize the change and impermanence constantly present in the world, insisting that even the self is not an ongoing entity but one that involves a constantly changing series of states. They seek to break free from this situation to achieve enlightenment.

Buddhism began with the teachings of Siddhartha Gautama (c.563-c.483 BCE), known as the Buddha (meaning Enlightened One). As a young man, he abandoned a life of luxury for a spiritual quest. He came to believe that all life was characterized by *dukkha*, meaning suffering, dissatisfaction or frustration. He accepted the common notion of a cycle of rebirth, but came to the conclusion that it is desire and attachment to the world which keep the cycle going. The Buddha is believed to have achieved enlightenment when he broke free of this desire.

Buddhism is in many ways an essentially practical religion. After his enlightenment, the Buddha traveled to spread his conclusions and to help others achieve enlightenment and thus enter Nirvana (the state beyond the cycle of rebirth). He refused to answer obtuse doctrinal questions, insisting instead on the need to search for spiritual truth and to live a compassionate life.

Buddhists generally seek to follow the 'eightfold path' of right understanding, right intention, right speech, right action, right livelihood, right effort, right mindfulness and right concentration. This is sometimes called the 'middle path', meaning that it is based on moderation, avoiding the extremes of indulgence and asceticism (this is often seen as a contrast with Jainism). Meditation is the central religious practice in many forms of Buddhism.

There are numerous varieties of Buddhism in today's world, although most can be grouped broadly into Theravada and Mahayana. The former is the most conservative about adherence to what are seen as the Buddha's original teachings, while the latter has tended to allow more innovation and development.

Buddhist ethics place a strong emphasis on compassion and nonviolence towards all living beings, usually including animals. This has often meant that Buddhists have been at the forefront of movements for peace and many have found that belief in equality sits easily with their faith. However, other Buddhists have willingly joined armies and, as with most religions, there are those who have justified wars in the name of Buddhism.

Although Buddhism developed in India, most Buddhists can now be found in China, Sri Lanka and southeast Asia. Buddhism has been increasingly popular in the West in recent decades; for example, it is now the largest non-Christian religion in Australia. There are thought to be about 400 million Buddhists in the world.

*Sikhism* also grew out of Hinduism but has developed as a distinct religion. Sikhism is closely identified with the Punjab, a region of northern India. Over 90 per cent of the world's 20 million Sikhs live in the Punjab, with sizeable communities also in Britain, Canada and the United States.

Sikhism began with the teachings of Guru Nanak (1469-1539) who was influenced by both Hinduism and Islam. After a strong internal experience of God, Nanak taught that inward spirituality and truthful action are more important than outward rituals. He emphasized the oneness of God, who reveals himself in creation but is distinct from humanity (not incarnate as in many Hindu traditions).

Unlike Hinduism, which has a vast number of gurus teaching various approaches, Sikhism gives the word 'guru' only to its highest leaders. God is 'the true guru' about whom Nanak and his successors taught. Nanak was the first of 10 human gurus, who each led the Sikh community in their time. While there has been no human guru since the death of Guru Gobind

---

## The Golden Rule

The principle that we should each treat others as we wish to be treated appears in varied forms across religions and cultures. Known technically as the Ethic of Reciprocity, it is more often referred to as the Golden Rule because it is fundamental to so many religions, as the following quotes demonstrate.

*'Do not do to others what would cause pain if done to you.'* Mahabharata

*'Do not do to others all that is not well for yourself.'* Avesta

*'One should treat all creatures in the world as one would like to be treated.'* Mahavira Vardhamana

*'Treat not others in ways that you yourself would find hurtful.'* The Buddha

*'Do not do to others what you do not want done to yourself.'* K'ung Tzu

*'Regard your neighbor's gain as your own gain and your neighbor's loss as your own loss.'* Lao Tzu

*'Do not do to others that which would anger you if others did it to you.'* Socrates

*'What is hateful to you, do not do your neighbor. This is the whole Law.'* Talmud

*'In everything, do to others as you would have them do to you.'* Jesus Christ

*'Not one of you truly believes until you wish for others what you wish for yourself.'* Muhammad

*'Treat others as you would be treated yourself.'* Guru Granth Sahib

*'Desire not for anyone the things you would not desire for yourself.'* Baha'u'llah ∎

## A religious world

Singh (1666-1708), Sikhs regard their scripture as the '11th guru'. It is known as Guru Granth Sahib and copies of the book as well as its contents are treated with reverence.

Sikhs give a high priority to hospitality. Sikh gurdwaras (or temples) are known for their *langar,* or free meals. The practice of *langar* exemplifies the Sikh belief in equality as everyone sits together on the floor to eat, with no regard to social status. Sikhism has a positive regard for other faiths and the gurus criticized the caste system, although attitudes to caste vary among Sikhs today. Similarly, some Sikhs have defended sexist attitudes while others have promoted equality and in some areas there has been significant progress in terms of the position of women.

The term *khalsa* refers to the community of fully initiated Sikhs, both male and female. Its members are marked by the 'five Ks' (because each word begins with a K in Punjabi): uncut hair, comb, breeches, bangle and sword (the latter usually small and symbolic).

### Religions deriving from East Asia

While East Asian religions are often overlooked in international discussion, this is surprising given their historical influence and number of adherents today. Chinese religion, in particular, has exercised a significant influence even outside China in the last century. Religion in China and Japan tends to have fluid boundaries, with many people belonging to more than one religious group or not distinguishing between them.

*Confucianism* is the oldest of the large religions founded in China. It derives from the teachings of K'ung Tzu (551-479 BCE), traditionally known in the West as Confucius. As a government official who became a religious teacher, he was keen to promote what he regarded as an ethical social order. Sayings attributed to him are contained in the Analects, a Confucian scripture.

The two key concepts in Confucianism are *jen* and *li*. Both these terms were familiar in China before K'ung Tzu, but he developed them into a philosophy that emphasized human relationships over ritual and speculation. *Jen* refers to virtue and compassion. *Li* is about behavior, which K'ung Tzu saw as more about ethics than ritual. He approached *jen* and *li* in a pragmatic rather than legalistic way.

When the two are related and implemented, he said, they form the basis of the 'five relationships'. The first is that between ruler and subject, with the principle being that the ruler should be benevolent and the subject loyal. Similarly, the parent should be kind and the child devoted. Similar approaches apply to relationships between husband and wife, between older brother and younger brother and between older friend and younger friend.

Thus a Confucian approach to society can be seen as paternalistic rather than egalitarian. However, K'ung Tzu encouraged compassion for all people and adapted the term *chun tzu*, meaning 'son of an aristocrat' to refer to a moral person of any background. It should be emphasized that Confucianism has developed in many ways and influenced varied schools of thought. For example, Meng Ke (371-288 BCE; known in the West as Mencius) taught that *jen* is innate and that humans have a natural ability to be good, which can be uncovered by inward contemplation and moral endeavor.

**Daoism** (also called Taoism), has obscure origins, but is related to the teachings of Lao Tzu, thought to have lived in the sixth century BCE. Many of its attitudes can be found in the scripture known as the Daodejing (or Tao Te Ching).

The key concept is Dao, often translated as 'The

Way'. Dao is the cosmic principle that allows all nature to function. It is the unchanging first principle that existed before the universe. The aim of the Daoist is to live in harmony with the Dao. Such harmony ensures appropriate conduct.

Many Daoists believe that this harmony can be achieved through a life of simplicity and self-control, involving meditation and a detachment from the world. Such practices are aided by the flow of *qi*, a term that refers to the breath of life or energy. The relative passivity of Daoism contrasts with Confucian notions of dutiful activity.

The concepts of *yin* and *yang* are central to Daoism and they appear in much other Chinese thought. They are the polar opposites at work in nature. *Yin* is associated with passivity, the female, night, coldness and the moon. *Yang* involves activity, the male, light, heat and the sun. The shifting balance between *yin* and *yang* determines the state of the natural world. Many Daoists also apply the concept to society, culture and politics and maintain that an appropriate balance is necessary for personal health and wellbeing. Several Chinese thinkers have even contrasted the passive *yin* of Daoism with the active *yang* of Confucianism.

Daoism's immersion in Chinese culture and fluid parameters means that it overlaps considerably with various other traditions, including Confucianism, Buddhism and earlier indigenous practices.

The Chinese tendency for blurred religious boundaries makes it difficult to measure either Confucians or Daoists. However, there are thought to be over 400 million people in the world practicing what is broadly described as Chinese traditional religion, including both these groups and others.

*Shinto*, the traditional religion of Japan, is affected by a similar blurring. It has developed alongside Japanese Buddhism and many Japanese people participate in both Shinto and Buddhist practices.

A key concept in Shinto is *kami*, meaning the spirit or spiritual essence of a particular place or entity. The word is sometimes translated as 'god', but kami are not gods as understood in South Asian or Abrahamic religions. For example, awe in nature may inspire reverence for kami, and valued individuals may be regarded as kami (usually after death). Abstract concepts – such as justice or beauty – may be kami also. While most kami are localized, some have a more national association, particularly Amaterasu, associated with the sun.

Shinto worship is usually focused on shrines. In addition to public shrines, smaller shrines in homes or even business premises are not uncommon. Purity – known as *kiyome* – is an important concept, with a number of practices aimed at purification. Spiritual salvation as such has little relevance to Shinto, which is often seen as a mainly material religion (this is complicated, however, by its mixing with Buddhism).

Shinto texts include Kojiki and Nihongi, deriving from the eighth century CE. They describe creation, kami and the divine origins of Japan. From the 19th century, Japanese authorities promoted the idea that the Emperor was a living kami but this idea fell from favor in the latter half of the 20th century. The fluid boundaries of Shinto make it very hard to state a number of adherents but its strong link with Japanese cultural traditions means it retains a secular importance for Japan as well as a religious one.

**Indigenous religions**
While much talk of religion focuses on 'world religions' that are followed across the globe, there are many people who follow more localized and small-scale traditions linked to their own lands. These religions are by their very nature enormously varied. While avoiding the temptation to exaggerate the similarities

between indigenous religions, it is possible to identify certain broad themes that are common to many (but by no means all) of them.

One of the most striking is the holistic approach of indigenous worldviews. They do not divide the sacred from the secular but see religion and spirituality as entirely natural and inseparable from the rest of life. This generally involves an understanding of spiritual forces that permeate and animate both living things and inanimate entities. Indigenous attitudes usually go further than respect for creation, seeing humans as but one part of an environment in which other animals and plants – not to mention rivers, mountains, forests and so on – have their part to play.

While involving a large number of spirits or divinities, many indigenous religions also recognize a High God, often called a Sky God or given a personal name. Many see the High God as remote from human affairs and are more prepared to interact with lesser divinities. For some, there is greater concentration on general spiritual power, sometimes referred to as *mana*, after its name in certain Pacific religions. For others, the High God is less remote, as in the Odinani religion of Nigeria. It should also be emphasized that not all indigenous groups have a High God.

As indigenous religions are by their nature linked to particular lands, there tend to be wide differences between groups in different areas or climates. For example, African indigenous religions in coastal areas may give a prominent place to divinities or spirits associated with the sea. These tend to be far less important for those living inland. Similarly, North American indigenous faiths in groups that have traditionally lived by hunting vary from those focused on farming. While they tend to share a reverence for animal life, this is manifested differently.

Many indigenous traditions are based around oral retelling of powerful stories that may hold a similar place to the scriptures of those religions that are more focused on writing. Although indigenous religions are usually ancient in their origins, this certainly does not mean that they do not change. Most have undergone considerable development over centuries. For example, Candomble, which is particularly popular in Brazil, derives from beliefs and practices brought there by African slaves in the 18th century and later influenced by Roman Catholicism.

This is an example of the ambiguous relationship of indigenous traditions to Christianity and Islam. Religions are frequently fused together and it is not uncommon for devout Christian faith to be combined with indigenous elements. Many have been keen to equate the High God of indigenous worldviews with the God of Abrahamic faiths, though some traditional indigenous practitioners regard such equation as invalid.

Several indigenous traditions involve shamanism,

---

### 'Cults' and the anti-cult movement

The word 'cult' is often used to describe a minority religious group, particularly of an exclusivist or fundamentalist variety. Members of the anti-cult movement apply the word to groups which they consider to be abusive towards their own members or towards others.

In general, however, the word is used far more loosely than this. A number of Christians use the term to describe groups which consider themselves to be Christian but which are not part of mainstream Christianity. For example, in Britain, lists of 'cults' generally include the Church of Jesus Christ of Latter-Day Saints, known as the Mormons. In the US, they are far less likely to do so. This is surely not unrelated to the fact that there are very few Mormons in Britain, while far higher numbers of Mormons have significant cultural and political influence in parts of the US.

While some campaigners are understandably concerned about manipulative practices in groups they call 'cults', the term's overuse means that it is now little more than a derogatory way to refer to religious minorities. Furthermore, when tackling religious abuse, there is a danger of seeing it only in groups labeled as 'cults' and thereby overlooking the abuse that can at times be found in mainstream religious organizations. ∎

a somewhat broad term that refers to a number of practices, although the word 'shaman' derives from the Tungus people of eastern Siberia. Broadly speaking, a shaman enters a trance state during which it is believed that he/she can experience a different dimension. Since the 20th century, this practice has become popular outside of traditional indigenous communities.

Indigenous religions are at their strongest in sub-Saharan Africa, Australasia, the Pacific Islands, North America and parts of South America. However, the mixing of indigenous practices with Muslim and Christian religion makes it difficult to count adherents. There is much debate over the validity or otherwise of speaking, for example, of 'Australian indigenous religion' or 'American indigenous religion', as this may overstate the similarities between varied groups. Some scholars argue that African religions differ from each other as much as they differ from indigenous religions in other parts of the world.

While there is much truth in this approach, cultural and political factors have led to an emphasis on regional similarities between indigenous religions. For example, those seeking to defend or revive indigenous traditions in North America often speak in broad terms about Native American religion and culture, contrasting it with the more influential alternatives of Christianity and secularism.

Similarly, there has been a rediscovery of indigenous traditions by people who have not grown up with them or have grown up with a mixture of indigenous and other practices. In some forms, this has involved a revival of traditions that have not been prominent for centuries. There are increasing numbers of Europeans identifying with Paganism, which can be seen as European indigenous religion and which gradually lost its dominant position during the first millennium.

Indigenous religions have often played an important

role in movements of resistance to colonialism, as they involve a people's own traditions apart from the influence of their colonizers. The oppressive treatment of indigenous peoples by imperial powers has usually involved a portrayal of indigenous religion as either evil or simplistic. It is sadly still common for certain commentators to see indigenous religions as primitive, while others seek to romanticize them.

## Secular worldviews

No consideration of religions in the world is complete without a look at those movements which do not define themselves as religions but often operate like them. There are certain ways of looking at the world, and of behaving as a group, that make their followers appear religious.

Certain forms of nationalism provide an example. Extreme nationalists effectively ascribe a sacred or transcendent quality to their country (usually defined in racial rather than geographical terms) and assume it has the highest call on their loyalty. This may be sustained by stories and understandings of the nation's past that perform a mythical function, along with rituals that include military marches or veneration of armed forces. This approach has been taken to its greatest lengths by Fascism and Nazism. The German leader Adolf Hitler (1889-1945) was revered by his followers to a degree that bordered on worship.

Juche, the state ideology of North Korea, looks very much like a religion, with some arguing that it should be included in global statistics on religious adherence. Developed by Kim Il-Sung (1912-94), it emphasizes political, economic and military independence for the country and now includes the principle of prioritizing the army. Military rituals and powerful stories about Korea's history and founders bear religious hallmarks and a godlike status is accorded to Kim Il-Sung and his successor Kim Jong-Il (1941- ). Juche took the place of Marxism in North Korean state philosophy.

Marxism itself is also frequently described as a secular religion. As developed by Karl Marx (1818-83) and others, Marxism provides a detailed analysis of the uneven distribution of wealth and power along with an approach to how this can be changed. While it would be stretching the point to see Marx's own teachings as a religion, certain governments that considered themselves Marxist have combined an almost spiritual hope for the future with devotion to leaders and sacred texts. In China in the latter years of Mao Zedong (1893-1976), the *Thoughts of Chairman Mao* effectively operated as scripture.

Certain attitudes in today's secular society can also be seen as religious when they appear to replace former religious hopes with alternative forms of faith. This point is often made in relation to rare individuals whose deaths provoke mass grief along with what amount to shrines and pilgrimage sites. Examples include the US singer Elvis Presley (1935-77) and also Diana Spencer (1961-97), a member of the British royal family. There have been suggestions that the level of trust some people place in medicine or in certain forms of psychotherapy replaces the religious faith of their ancestors. However, it is probably more accurate to say that such things have taken the place of elements of religion rather than that they are wholesale alternatives to religion.

There is a complicated question when it comes to secular humanism, whose supporters place humanity at the center of their worldview and regard humans' needs and rights as their primary concern. Not only has this position been thought through and chosen by many, but it can also be seen more broadly as the dominant worldview in many Western countries today. The most extreme secular humanists believe that only science and reason can be sources of truth and that religion is necessarily negative in its effects.

Such views have been popularized in recent years by 'New Atheists' such as Richard Dawkins (1941- ). There is considerable debate over the political and cultural implications of regarding secular humanism or New Atheism as religious positions.

The controversies relating to such movements often involve argument not only on the nature of religion but on the nature of truth, and on how religion relates to science, history and other approaches to the world. It is these questions to which we turn next.

# 3 Questions of truth

**What does it mean to say that a religion is true? Questions of truth are central to much discussion of religion, but the questions themselves are as varied as the answers.**

OUR PERCEPTIONS OF truth owe at least as much to personal experience and cultural context as to verifiable facts. Many issues of ethics and politics cannot be settled simply by appealing to impartial assessment of the evidence. Nonetheless, it is common in the West today for 'truth' to be used as a synonym for 'fact'. This implies that truth is uncomplicated: something is either true or it is not. However, it is inaccurate to regard religions as competing sets of factual claims. Religious notions of truth predate our society's tendency to equate truth with fact.

The factual approach to truth is often linked with science. Science has clearly brought immeasurable benefits to humanity, as well as being used to fuel war and environmental destruction. It is popularly seen as a process through which people carry out impartial observations in order to reach theories with general application on the basis of the evidence. However, many scientists accept that science is not as objective as is sometimes thought. A scientist will be affected by his/her own background, education and views, even if he/she is determined to be as unbiased as possible. Scientists' theories inevitably build partly on observations made by others and are presented in the type of language considered acceptable to the scientific enterprise.

To overlook bias and subjectivity would be to suggest that science operates within a vacuum. Ignoring cultural, political and economic contexts is as dangerous with science as with religion. A deeper understanding of reality recognizes science as one of the most important ways of approaching and uncovering truth and making a difference to the world. But it is not the only one. Science is extremely helpful for diagnosing diseases and predicting the next eclipse. It is considerably less useful for understanding the nature of love or appreciating a powerful piece of music. Those who attempt to analyze religions as if they were sets of scientific claims are thus making a category error.

## Experience and behavior

Experience is the basis for much of what we regard as true on an everyday basis – truth comes through sight, sound, smell, feeling and taste before it comes through reason or science. Our different experiences are to some extent responsible for our different understandings of truth. In turn, cultural and political factors play a major role in determining which experiences we are likely to have.

It is therefore unsurprising that many approaches to truth, along with many religions, are more concerned with behavior than belief. For example, the Akhan people of Thailand practice a religion and tradition known as Zan. The researcher Deborah Tooker found a strong uniformity of religious practice amongst them along with a wide diversity of contradictory statements on their beliefs. It is their practice, not their belief, that defines their religion. Tooker found no-one who had been excluded from the community because of their beliefs, but some had been excluded because they did not 'do Zan'.[1] In such contexts, religious truth is more about behaving in certain ways than it is about believing in factual statements.

Most religions have been founded by people who underwent a major experience of the divine, either at a single moment or over a longer period. Zoroaster spread his message after his experience allowed him to know God 'in truth'. The Buddha attained enlightenment after years of searching, Muhammad encountered the angel Gabriel, Guru Nanak felt swept into God's presence, Baha'ullah experienced a revelation from God about his future role in the world. For some, these were positive experiences in which they felt blessed and united with the divine. Others, such as Muhammad and many of the Jewish prophets, initially resisted their experiences, repelled by the role to which they felt called.

For many of those who undergo such experiences, truth is something to be experienced rather than simply worked out. Nonetheless, there are clearly dangers in basing truth too much on individual experience. The Jewish fundamentalist Yigal Amir, who assassinated the Israeli Prime Minister Yitzhak Rabin in 1994, claimed to be acting 'on orders from God'.[2] Several religious groups have sought to address this problem by balancing individual experience against other considerations. For example, Sufi Muslims place a high value on spiritual experience, but it is expected to be in accordance with the Qur'an. Rastafarians and Quakers use methods of collective discernment to allow the community to test an individual's leading.

Many emphasize that experiential truth is a deep matter that requires effort, reflection and commitment beyond momentary flashes of insight. Within many religions, there are movements committed to the possibility of deep and direct contact between the individual and the divine. Such movements are often described as mystical, although at times the word is inaccurately used to suggest esotericism and irrelevance. However, mystics generally emphasize that theirs is not a simplistic or easy approach, but one that requires discipline, self-awareness, considerable effort and a sense of humility in the face of the mysteries of the universe.

This humble approach to truth contrasts with the

certainty that some religious adherents undoubtedly display. It is well worth remembering that their claims to certainty are at odds with much religious teaching over many traditions and centuries. Indeed, there have always been those who regarded too much certainty as blasphemous, on the grounds that it implied that a human could share divine knowledge. 'My thoughts are not your thoughts,' declares God in the Hebrew Bible, 'Nor are your ways my ways'.[3] The Vedas, which are central to Hinduism, are frequently quoted to promote caution on questions of truth:

> Who then knows whence it has arisen,
> Whence this emanation hath arisen,
> Whether God disposed it, or whether
> he did not,
> Only he who is its overseer in highest
> heaven knows.
> Or perhaps he does not know![4]

Despite the diversity of experience, mysticism is usually related to a rejection of self-centeredness. Many mystics have discovered an essential unity with both the divine and the rest of humanity, and often with the rest of creation, which leads them to take a strongly compassionate approach to the world. Mystics tend to identify truth with behavior more than with beliefs.

Mysticism threatens authority precisely because it challenges the right of any one individual or institution to declare what is true. Mystics have frequently been suppressed by religious leaders, particularly within the Abrahamic religions. After years of mystical practice, the Muslim teacher al-Husayn ibn Mansur al-Hallaj felt so united with God and the Truth that he was able to say, 'I am the Real', a statement that contributed to the reasons for his execution by the Baghdad authorities in 922.

## Questions of truth

### Language and narrative

The perception of truth as straightforward and factual is contradicted by the everyday use of metaphor and narrative for purposes of explanation and dialogue. The choice of language, the meaning of a word or the context of a saying can make a big difference, even more so in religion than in life as a whole. We have only to look at the hotly fought controversies over the correct translation of scriptures to realize that a conflict about truth in religion may be centered on a dispute about language and what it means.

Take for example the Arabic word *kufr*, found in the Qur'an. Often rendered as something like 'unbelief' or 'faithlessness', it is used today by certain Muslims in a very casual way to describe anyone who is not a Muslim. This allows them to see the Qur'an's comments on *kufr* as justification for aggressive hostility to non-Muslims. In contrast, other Muslims, such as the theologian Farid Esack, suggest that the word more accurately refers to an active rejection of God and an obstruction of justice rather than the members of any particular group. His analysis of linguistic nuances in the Qur'an contributes to his conclusion that 'it is not labels that are counted by God, but actions that are weighed'.[5]

Even when dealing only in one language, many religious expressions can be so controversial and contested that they assume wildly different meanings according to who is using them. A number of theologians suggest that the word 'God' is used in an unduly straightforward way in modern religion. Most monotheistic religions have in the past been keen to emphasize that God's existence is beyond existence as humans understand it; God does not simply exist *in addition* to people, animals and objects, but underpins them all. This point is today reiterated by writers who argue that religious adherents who use the word 'God' in too unthinking a way unintentionally give fuel to critics of religion who attack it as simplistic.

Words also assume different meanings depending on context and experience. A preacher who says that 'God is our father' is likely to trigger a different reaction from someone whose father is loving and affectionate than from someone whose father is bullying or abusive. Further, the context in which a phrase is originally spoken or written may well be different from the context in which it is later used. Most religious leaders in the Abrahamic traditions deny that God is literally either male or female, but are reluctant to call God 'she' rather than 'he'. Some see this as part of a feminist agenda while their opponents consider them to be motivated by sexism. This is not a new debate. In the fourth century, the Christian bishop Gregory of Nyssa (331-395) argued that it was as acceptable to call God either 'mother' or 'father', insisting that: 'Both terms mean the same, because the divine is neither male nor female'.[6]

At the opposite end of the spectrum from factual truth are those who suggest that truth would not exist without language. A number of thinkers argue that we can only create truth for ourselves through our own language and community. This position, which can broadly be described as non-realism, is not a rejection of the notion of truth, but rather of objective truth. To many non-realists, if a community believes that God exists and consider themselves to experience this existence, then *God really exists*. However, he does not exist objectively. He would not exist if the community ceased to exist.

This extreme interpretation of truth may be confined to a small minority of religious adherents but it has been influential in academic circles. It is opposed by many others who suggest that it is a big leap from the recognition that humans cannot be fully objective about truth to the belief that nothing at all is objectively real. Such people recognize the subjectivity of language and thought without rejecting the notion of an objective reality 'out there'. The realization that all language is subjective and biased is important. Even an attempt to write an unbiased account of an incident or a controversy will be affected by the writer's own unconscious assumptions about which factors are important enough to include.

Religious thinkers have generally recognized this when they have emphasized the importance of myth. Unfortunately, the word 'myth' is now often used to mean something untrue, but a more sophisticated meaning of the word refers to a narrative which conveys an understanding of truth without necessarily being factual. Anyone who has read a powerful novel, or been deeply affected by a film, can testify that a fictional account can convey a truthful point. The meaning of a myth goes beyond its content and is primarily about the context in which it is used. Karen Armstrong gives the example of the *Enuma Elish,* a Babylonian myth dating to over three and a half millennia ago:

> *The gods met at Babylon, the center of the new earth, and built a temple where the celestial rites could be performed. The result was the great ziggurat... and the gods... performed the liturgy from which the universe receives its structures... The myth expresses the inner meaning of civilization, as the Babylonians saw it. They knew perfectly well that their own ancestors had built the ziggurat but the story of the Enuma Elish articulated their belief that their creative enterprise could only endure if it partook of the power of the divine.*[7]

Myths may or may not contain literal and factual truth, but this is not the point of them. Attempts to understand them in this way ignore the intention behind them and create controversies about issues that may well be less important than the points that the myth is intended to make. Let's take the statement 'Jesus walked on water', a claim made in the New Testament. The story dates to a time when the power of water was a frequent symbol of the unpredictable dangers of nature, which only God could control. The writers knew that their readers would understand that they were claiming Jesus had powers given to him by God. Of course, it is quite possible that they also believed that Jesus *literally* walked on water, but the question would have bothered them far less than it concerns many people today.

This is not to say that there is no issue of truth to be engaged with. Someone who does not believe Jesus had powers from God may well reject the story altogether, finding it untrue in every sense. However, to understand the nature of truth claims in religion,

---

### Interfaith dialogue

Recent decades have seen a growth in organized interfaith dialogue, through which people of different religions seek to learn about and understand each other. More recently, there have been attempts to include non-religious people in such dialogue. For some, these processes are a matter of seeking truth together. For others, they are simply about people finding out what they have in common and seeking to understand each other. The Japanese Christian Kosuke Koyama identified the need for such an approach in the 1970s:

'I found that the study of *ist* is far more interesting than that of *ism*. I carefully observed Buddhists and to my surprise found many similar things between them and myself. One day I said to myself: "We are just alike. We want money. We want position. We want honor. We are both concerned about ourselves. We are failing to practice what the Buddha or Christ commanded. We are quick in judging others and very slow in judging ourselves!" Comparisons on the level of Budd*hist* and Christ*ian* often produce an embarrassing result. On the contrary we can be well sheltered when we engage in the comparison between Budd*hism* and Christ*ianity*.' ∎

Kosuke Koyama, *Waterbuffalo Theology* (SCM Press, 1974)

it is important that we understand what it is that is being claimed. In this example, the point of the story has been missed by those who deride it as unscientific, those who stridently assert its literalism and people who try to 'de-mythologize' it by suggesting that Jesus was only walking *near* the water.

It is not only religious groups who use myths, promoting narratives whose meaning is more about context than content. Militant atheists look back at historical controversies between scientists and religious authorities – such as Galileo and the Roman Church, or Charles Darwin and the Christian establishment – as heroic occasions on which science took on religion, rather than considering other factors at play.

### Fundamentalism and exclusive truth

The complexity of truth is denied by two movements which have gained ground in recent years. The first is fundamentalism. Although the word is often used as a synonym for extremism, it is far more specific. Fundamentalism is a peculiarly modern movement, having arisen at the beginning of the 20th century as a backlash against what some saw as the compromises made by religious groups with secularism and liberalism. Fundamentalist groups can now be found within most religions. They tend to believe that their religion's leadership has sold out and that they have a duty to preserve their faith.

Central to the fundamentalists' approach is the conviction that only their religion or worldview has the truth. Other religions are regarded as false and often as evil. The British Christian fundamentalist Colin Urquhart has suggested that non-Christian religions are inspired by the Devil.[8] The Egyptian Muslim fundamentalist Sayyid Abu Ala Mawdudi insisted that there is 'only one way' for 'the entire human race' and therefore that no religion other than Islam can be acceptably practiced by anyone.[9]

Those who take such a view are of course unlikely to engage in dialogue with people of other faiths or of none, unless it is in an attempt to convert them. The right-wing British Christian David Holloway criticizes interfaith dialogue on the grounds that truth 'has all to do with facts' and 'all claims... cannot be right'.[10] It must be admitted that there are those who give the impression that there is nothing problematic about believing that religions are all simultaneously true. In reality, however, most of those who engage seriously in interfaith dialogue are more likely to be seeking truth together, with agreement on some issues and honest, respectful disagreement on others.

In the same way that religious fundamentalists refuse to see anything good or truthful in any religion but their own, there is a form of atheist fundamentalism that refuses to see anything good or truthful in *any* religion. The writer Martin Amis insists that 'a religion is a belief-system with no basis in reality whatever'.[11] Such rhetoric is common amongst a small group of influential writers and scientists commonly dubbed the 'New Atheists'. This movement developed in the first decade of the 21st century, pioneered by the British biologist Richard Dawkins, whose 2006 book *The God Delusion* became an international bestseller.

Just as religious fundamentalists accuse many members of their religions of having sold out, so the New Atheists attack other atheists for being insufficiently hostile to religion. Dawkins condemns atheists who are positive about faith as 'vicarious second-order believers'. He refuses to be positive about progressive elements within religion, claiming that 'moderate religion' is an 'open invitation to extremism'.[12] Such comments are very similar to the rhetoric that religious fundamentalists use about faiths other than their own. For example, when the right-wing British Christian Jon Gower Davies claims that 'there are no moderate Muslims'[13] he sounds remarkably similar to the American New Atheist Sam Harris, who makes the sweeping assertion that 'most Muslims are utterly deranged by their religious faith.'[14]

It seems that most atheists do not support the militant secularism of Dawkins and Amis. New Atheism is no more representative of atheism generally than Islamic fundamentalism is of Islam, or Christian fundamentalism of Christianity. The atheist philosopher Ronald Aronson has criticized the 'emptiness' of the New Atheist approach, insisting that 'living without God means turning toward something'.[15] The Marxist scholar Terry Eagleton is very critical of the 'bigotry, superstition, wishful thinking and oppressive ideology' associated with religion, but argues that religion as attacked by the New Atheists is 'a worthless caricature of the real thing, rooted in a degree of ignorance and prejudice to match religion's own'.[16]

While the New Atheists demonstrate a simplistic understanding of truth, many religious people will nonetheless share their horror at the atrocities perpetrated in the name of religion. Perhaps the most persuasive section of Dawkins' book is his passionate attack on religious homophobia.

However, the New Atheists' ability to tackle such abuses is hampered by their exclusive approach to truth. The leading New Atheist Christopher Hitchens is so determined to insist that religion can never inspire anything good that he claims the American civil rights activist Martin Luther King (1929-68) was a Christian only in a 'nominal sense' rather than a 'real' one. The briefest glance at Luther King's writings, let alone a more detailed study, reveals the importance of his faith in inspiring and sustaining his commitment to nonviolent struggle. On the other hand, when it is pointed out that while many tyrants have been motivated by religion, others – such as Stalin and

Hitler – have not, Hitchens claims that Nazism and Stalinism are examples of 'political religion'.[17] It is not hard to come to the conclusion that Hitchens regards almost anything he opposes as 'religion' and anything he approves of as 'not religion'. Such an approach does not make for an effective struggle against injustice.

## Power and privilege

Both religious fundamentalists and New Atheists tend to have a literal approach to religious texts. The American Christian fundamentalist Jerry Falwell described the Bible as 'absolutely infallible... in areas such as geography, science, history, etc'.[18] Richard Dawkins argues that religions make 'the same kinds of claims that scientists make, except they're usually false'.[19]

---

### Creation stories

Christian fundamentalists strongly defend biblical creation narratives as literal accounts, but when interpreted on a deeper and less literal level they have inspired a far more progressive outlook. The 17th century English radical Gerard Winstanley pointed out that neither property nor inequality appeared in God's original creation:

'In the beginning of time, the great Creator... made the Earth to be a common Treasury... not one word was spoken in the beginning that one branch of mankind should rule over another...

'But... selfish imagination taking possession... did set up one man to teach and rule over another, and thereby the Spirit was killed, and man was brought into bondage, and became a greater slave to such of his own kind, than the beasts of the field were to him... And that Earth that is within this Creation, made a common storehouse for all, is bought and sold, and kept in the hands of a few, whereby the great Creator is mightily dishonored, as if he were a respector of persons, delighting in the comfortable livelihood of some, and rejoicing in the miserable poverty and straits of others. From the beginning it was not so.' ∎

Gerard Winstanley, 'The True Levellers' Standard Advanced' [1649] in *Radical Christian Writings: A Reader*, edited by Andrew Bradstock and Christopher Rowland (Blackwell Publishers, 2002). [Spellings modernized]

---

## Questions of truth

Protestant fundamentalists reject evolution because it contradicts their interpretation of the opening chapters of the Book of Genesis, at the beginning of the Bible. But for most of history, the literalism of Genesis was not an issue. Prominent Christian theologians such as John Calvin (1509-64), one of the most influential thinkers in the history of Protestantism, suggested that these narratives were not literal. Even when Charles Darwin (1809-82) caused controversy by publishing his theories on evolution, religious leaders who objected generally did so on the grounds that Darwinism seemed to lower the status of humanity, rather than because of a literal interpretation of scriptural creation narratives. By equating truth with scientific fact, fundamentalists are buying into the modern secular outlook that they see themselves as opposing.

Several writers therefore suggest that fundamentalism and New Atheism are both due to a failure to recognize the validity of non-factual truth. The conflict between them has been described as a 'literalists' war'.[20] Armstrong argues that both movements are rooted in a failure to distinguish between *logos* and *mythos* – that is, between reason and science on the one hand and myth, art and imagination on the other. She suggests that modern society has forgotten the need for *mythos* and is trying to approach religion as if it were science.[21]

Literalism is undoubtedly a major factor in the rise of fundamentalism and New Atheism, but in order to understand these phenomena more fully, we need to consider questions of power and politics. It is helpful here to look at some of the disputes that are commonly portrayed as conflicts between religion and science.

The controversy between Galileo Galilei (1564-1642) and the Roman Catholic Church is a good example. The Pope at the time, Urban VIII (1568-1644), had shown a strong belief in the importance of scientific research. Galileo showed no sign of disbelieving in Christianity. The major conflict came in 1632 when Galileo published a thinly veiled defense of Copernicanism, a view that placed the sun rather than the Earth at the center of the universe. The Church had previously declared Copernicanism to be both scientifically false and heretical. Galileo's book was a challenge to their authority.

Urban VIII's priority was the position of the Church. The religious and political power structures over which he presided depended on the Church holding ultimate authority to declare what was true and what was not. The issue of a sun-centered universe was not *in itself* what outraged the Church authorities. Rather, they were threatened by someone working out truth independently of – and contrary to – their own teachings. We may admire Galileo for bravely standing up to an oppressive authority and asserting his own discoveries of truth. But the idea that this was a conflict between religion and science would have made no sense to either Galileo or Urban VIII.

Issues of politics and power are also important when we look at recent disputes about evolution. The theory of evolution by natural selection split both the scientific establishment and religious authorities in the 19th century. Evolution gradually became accepted in most of the world, before fresh controversies made the news towards the end of the 20th century and into the 21st. The disputes were particularly strong in the United States, where evolution has never been as widely accepted as in most other countries. The 1960s saw the beginnings of campaigns for the teaching of 'creation science' in schools. This is a supposedly scientific explanation of the world's origins that is linked to a literal – and biased – interpretation of the opening chapters of Genesis. By the turn of the century, 'creation science' had largely been replaced by 'intelligent design', a less explicitly Christian argument that suggests a personal designer rather than a coincidental process of evolution.

These movements are often backed both politically and financially by Christian churches. The struggle against evolution is frequently mentioned by Christian campaigners in the same breath as they talk of the need to defend the status of Christianity in the US. Theirs is a defensive argument, often aided by right-wing politicians seeking support from these conservatively Christian voters. In other words, this dispute is as much political as religious.

This situation highlights a key reason for the rise of both fundamentalism and New Atheism. Fundamentalism tends to develop from fear of a religion losing its social status or political position. Hindu fundamentalists fear the influence of religions such as Islam and Christianity in India. Islamic fundamentalists are clearly afraid of Muslims being influenced by 'Western' political ideas. The decline of Church power in several Western countries has led to calls for a return to a 'Christian nation'. The British fundamentalist group Christian Voice claims to speak for Christians 'who have had enough of secularist politicians imposing wickedness on the rest of us'.[22]

In the same way, New Atheism has followed a fear on the part of secularists that religion is regaining lost ground. In the 1960s and 1970s it looked as if religion could be on the way out in many Western societies, but by the 1990s, religious activism was experiencing a revival. Following the attacks on New York and Washington in 2001, and the subsequent 'war on terror', religion became a far more central topic of political and media discourse in western Europe.

Of course, writers such as Dawkins and Hitchens have fueled these debates. A number of Christian writers have written books in response to them, arguing for the existence of God. Most of these writers, such as Keith Ward and Alistair McGrath, are moderately conservative Christians rather than fundamentalists. However, they seem to accept many of the New Atheists' premises. They argue for God on rationalist grounds and they make limited reference to the political and social contexts that influence decisions about religion. In addition, they often play down the religious atrocities that Dawkins and his allies attack.

The Catholic feminist scholar Tina Beattie argues that both parties in this debate are concerned with 'the preoccupations of a minority of predominantly male Western thinkers'. She sees similarities between writers such as Dawkins and the Victorian European scholars who described what they saw as the 'primitive' practices of indigenous religions. She suggests that:

> *The new atheists have hardly moved on from that imperial world in which cultures dominated by a white male élite remain caught up in a territorial battle of colonization and conquest... If we want to understand how 'religion' functions in the world according to Dawkins, then we need to situate him in the context of those 19th-century scholars who perceived themselves as beacons of progress in a world of seething ignorance and barbarism. Like them, the new atheists labor under the delusion of their own superior knowledge.*[23]

The tendency of certain New Atheists to adopt a dismissive attitude to humanity is also highlighted by Eagleton, who refers to the 'cultural supremacism' of those 'who sneer at religion from the Senior Common Room window as yet more evidence of the thick-headedness of the masses'.[24] In fairness, it should be noted that some New Atheists exhibit this tendency far less than others, just as not all of them have backed war or promoted prejudice. Dawkins himself was a vocal opponent of the invasion of Iraq in 2003.

However, Hitchens gave it his enthusiastic support, while Amis describes the 'Islamic world' as 'less evolved' than the West. In 2001, he openly called for severe restrictions on Muslims' civil liberties.

The reality is that questions of truth cannot be considered aside from issues of power and politics. People campaigning against the powerful have frequently taken an unconventional approach to truth. A prime example is Mohandas Gandhi (1869-1948), the key figure behind nonviolent struggles for India's independence from the British empire. For Gandhi, truth is something to be lived out. To describe his approach, he coined the phrase *satyagraha*, often translated as 'truth force' or 'soul force'. As the writer Terrence J Rynne puts it:

> *Truth... is not just a cognitive affair but the goal of all human endeavors. We are made for the truth. We pine and long for the truth... To be in touch with the truth, or to use one of Gandhi's favorite expressions, to be 'attuned' to the truth, means therefore that you have the power of the universe working with you... For Gandhi, therefore, truth was a matter of living and acting in a way that relieved humanity of its burdens. One finds the truth only in service of people... Truth is latent until it is embodied in action. For Gandhi truth is to be discovered and created, found and enacted.*[25]

Such understandings of truth undermine the simplistic approach of fundamentalists, New Atheists and all those who want to reduce truth to questions of fact without regard to politics or culture. They are a reminder that to tackle the injustice and oppression which are often associated with religion, we need to go deeper than religion's casual critics are prepared to go.

**1** Cited by Malory Nye, *Religion* (Routledge, 2008). **2** Cited by Oliver McTernan, *Violence in God's Name* (Darton, Longman and Todd, 2003). **3** Isaiah 55,8 *The Bible, New Revised Standard Version* (Cambridge University Press, 1993). **4** RC Zaehner, *Hindu Scriptures* (Everyman's Library, 1992). **5** Farid Esack, *Qur'an, Liberation and Pluralism* (Oneworld Publishers, 1997). **6** Cited by Adrian Thatcher, *Liberating Sex* (SPCK, 1993). **7** Karen Armstrong, *A History of God* (Vintage Books, 1993). **8** Cited by Karen Armstrong, op cit. **9** Cited by Malise Ruthven, *Fundamentalism* (Oxford University Press, 2007). **10** David Holloway, *Church and State in the New Millennium* (Harper Collins, 2000). **11** Martin Amis, 'The Voice of the Lonely Crowd' in *The Guardian*, 1 June 2002. **12** Richard Dawkins, *The God Delusion* (Black Swan, 2006). **13** Jon Gower Davies, *In Search of the Moderate Muslim* (Social Affairs Unit, 2009). **14** Sam Harris, *Letter to a Christian Nation* (Bantam Press, 2007). **15** Ronald Aronson, *Living Without God* (Counterpoint, 2008). **16** Terry Eagleton, *Reason, Faith and Revolution: Reflections on the God debate* (Yale University Press, 2009). **17** Christopher Hitchens, *God is Not Great* (Atlantic Books, 2007). **18** Jerry Falwell, *Finding Inner Peace and Strength* (Doubleday, 1982). **19** Richard Dawkins, *The God Delusion* (Black Swan, 2006). **20** Frank Schaeffer, 'A Literalists' War' in *Third Way*, September 2009. **21** Karen Armstrong, *The Case for God* (The Bodley Head, 2009). **22** Christian Voice website, www.christianvoice.org.uk/abouthim.html; accessed 7 August 2009. **23** Tina Beattie, *The New Atheists* (Darton, Longman and Todd, 2007). **24** Terry Eagleton, *Reason, Faith and Revolution: Reflections on the God debate* (Yale University Press, 2009). **25** Terrence J Rynne, *Gandhi and Jesus: The saving power of nonviolence* (Orbis Books, 2008).

# 4 Power and oppression

**Powerful people have for centuries used religion to defend their position and to justify control of society, wealth and personal relationships. One of the most common reasons for the rejection of religion is its relationship to tyranny, violence, sexism, racism or homophobia.**

AT THE SAME time, religion has inspired and empowered some of the most effective campaigns for peace and social justice. However, we cannot consider religion and liberation without also considering religion and oppression.

Anyone seeking examples of this link does not need to look very far. Take the popular English Christian hymn *All Things Bright and Beautiful*, written in 1848 by Cecil Frances Alexander. Its most controversial verse is nowadays often omitted:

> *The rich man in his castle,*
> *The poor man at his gate,*
> *God made them, high or lowly,*
> *And ordered their estate.*[1]

In portraying the English class hierarchy as a God-given part of creation, Alexander contributed to a long tradition of giving religious blessing to inequality and injustice.

### Cause and effect

There are many different understandings of the relationship between religion and oppression. At one extreme are those who argue that religion is the *cause* of injustices. This view is common amongst the New Atheists, who have revived extreme anti-religious views in recent years. For example, Christopher Hitchens argues that: 'Religion makes people do wicked things they wouldn't ordinarily do... The licenses for genocide, slavery, racism are all right there in the holy text.'[2]

Others (including many atheists) criticize such an approach as simplistic, as it implies that there would be no injustice without religion and therefore ignores economic and political contexts. The opposite opinion is that religion is merely an *excuse* for injustices, which would be likely to happen anyway for other reasons. This view could also be said to make the relationship too simple. However, it is worth looking at a more sophisticated adaptation of this view, which suggests that religion tends to justify or promote injustices that exist for social and economic reasons. This approach was developed by Karl Marx, the first atheist philosopher to develop a convincing critique of religion's link with power and wealth.

Marx saw history as characterized by struggles for power between different classes, that is, groups with shared economic interests. Whichever class controls the economy controls society. Under capitalism, power is concentrated in the hands of a small minority who accumulate ownership of nearly all wealth.

While some of Marx's ideas may now be seen as misplaced, the accuracy of many of his predictions is staggering. He foresaw the ongoing decline of small and medium-sized businesses, the rise of transnational corporations and the globalization of economic power.

In Marx's thought, economics are the root of other aspects of life, including power, culture – and religion. Thus the form religion takes is dependent on the economic and class structures of the society in which it appears. He described the role of religion under capitalism:

*The wretchedness of religion is at once an expression of, and a protest against, real wretchedness. Religion is the sigh of the oppressed creature, the heart of a heartless world, the soul of soulless conditions. It is the opium of the people.*[3]

For Marx, religion is a way in which people cope with their suffering. He also saw that the ruling classes make use of religion for their own ends. He was well aware that it was not long since Christian monarchs in Europe had claimed to rule by a 'divine right' through which God had anointed their lineage. In Japan, it was not until 1989 that the Emperor formally renounced his claim to divinity.

Marx's view is not a conspiracy theory. He did not suggest that religion had been deliberately manufactured to fool the people. Rather, he saw religion as an aspect of ideology – a way of thinking and understanding the world that fits in with certain economic and political interests. He argued that religion diverts attention from socio-economic reality and ends up propping up or excusing inequality even when no-one explicitly sets out with this aim.

Many of the ways in which this happens are more subtle than the supposed divine anointing of monarchy or the casual snobbery of Alexander's hymn. For example, many (but by no means all) Evangelical Protestant groups focus almost exclusively on the conviction that anyone who accepts Christ can live in paradise for eternity. In several such groups, many members are from the poorer sectors of society, as the doctrine can be especially encouraging for people with few opportunities in life. However, by their excessive emphasis on the afterlife, such groups effectively discourage their members from acting to improve the world they live in now, thus helping to perpetuate the injustices they suffer.

Marx did not advocate the suppression of religion (unlike many later groups regarded as Marxist).

Rather, he expected it to wither away. End injustice and religion would gradually disappear.

While Marx's analysis is very helpful, it raises as many questions as it answers. His view of power relations has been attacked for giving insufficient consideration to matters other than economics. Most obviously, he fails to deal adequately with the diversity of cultures and religions that can exist within the same society, including religious movements which oppose the dominant powers and concern themselves with political and economic justice.

## Conflict and culture

Somebody able to consider the challenges raised by Marx's approach to society and culture was Antonio Gramsci (1891-1937), who spent 11 years of his life imprisoned for his beliefs in Mussolini's Italy. Fortunately for us, this gave him plenty of time to produce a phenomenal body of writing that took a basically Marxist approach to society while being more nuanced than Marx's own.

In every society, said Gramsci, certain aspects of culture, language and religion are dominant. They tend to be identified with the ruling classes and be seen as having the most value. Other forms exist, but are regarded as less important. Gramsci spoke of the 'hegemony' that promotes the preferred culture, language and religion of the wealthy and the powerful.

We can find a good example in 19th century Wales. The most affluent and influential people generally belonged to the established Anglican Church and communicated in English. In contrast, the Non-Conformist churches appealed to poorer parts of society and tended to worship in Welsh. The powerful were powerful for economic reasons, not because they were Anglican and English-speaking. However, these factors were marks of their status and allowed them to mix and communicate with other people of their own class. Non-Conformist Welsh speakers who were looking for social advancement were likely both to learn English and to consider a change of church.

At the same time, the continued existence of Non-Conformist churches played a major role in preserving the Welsh language and also provided a forum in which progressive ideas could spread. This is an example of what Gramsci called 'counter-hegemony', in which certain aspects of culture and religion conflict with the interests and preferences of the ruling class, but tend not to be as powerful as those that conform to them.

Similar examples of hegemony and counter-hegemony can be drawn from almost every society. Ideas and practices which go against the hegemony, while not necessarily suppressed, may be sidelined or ignored. In many countries, religious minorities face a marginalization that is sustained by the perpetuation of negative images and stereotypes.

In Britain, for example, parts of the media are explicitly hostile to Muslims. Despite Muslims' marginal position (they make up about three per cent of the UK population), certain newspapers suggest that they are enjoying privileges. For example, in 2008 the *Daily Star* ran a front-page story claiming that the BBC was biased towards Islam, using the headline 'BBC puts Muslims above you'.[4] Their choice of language is significant. The use of 'you' implies that no-one reading the newspaper is Muslim and thus that Muslims are a group apart from the public in general.

These attitudes are often linked with an assumption – found in many countries – that certain religions are somehow foreign, or at least new. This often applies even when a religion has been practiced in a country for some considerable time. For example, Sikhs have been present in Canada since at least the 1890s, and Muslims since at least the census of 1871, but in media discussion they are commonly associated only with much more recent immigration. In reality, such prejudices often reveal more about the culture in which they are promoted than they do about the group being discussed. In medieval western Europe, where the Church taught sexual purity, Islam was commonly portrayed as sexually licentious. In western Europe today, where a high value is placed on sexual freedom, Islam is regarded as sexually repressive. This is a striking example of the way in which counter-hegemonic cultures and religions are portrayed as alien, with little regard to their real nature.

## Domesticating danger

If we really want to understand how religion so often ends up linked with oppression, we need to look *within* religions. The dynamics of hegemony and counter-hegemony are very relevant here.

Hegemonic ideas within religious groups are often officially entrenched in doctrine and approved practice, while the counter-hegemony is more informal. As the Jewish feminist Leila Gal Berner puts it:

> *Jewish women have cultivated a religious 'folk' tradition replete with chants, songs, special recitations, and ritual objects... While kneading bread, or chopping vegetables, while giving birth and nursing their young, Jewish women called out to God, voices raised in supplication, dialogue, and communion. Through the centuries, however, women's heartfelt voices raised in song and celebration have generally been ignored by the male shapers of Jewish tradition.*[5]

Similar points could be made about the position of women within many other religious groups. Women

---

**Religion and sexuality**

'When we started Changing Attitude Nigeria in 2005, the first reaction I received from Archbishop Akinola was... a smear campaign against me. What is my crime? My crime is that I said I was a gay Nigerian Anglican who is tired of living in the closet over my sexuality...

'Why was the Church of Nigeria so angry with me? They were angry with me because at that time Archbishop Akinola, in collaboration with his western conservative friends, was saying that there were no homosexuals in Nigeria. My coming out showed their false claims up for what they were...

'I have repeatedly told Archbishop Akinola and his allies that what Westerners introduced to Nigeria was the Christian faith and homophobia. Homosexuality has existed in Africa from the beginning.' ■
Davis Mac-Iyalla

Davis Mac-Iyalla, 'No Change in Attitudes', *Guardian* website, 22 March 2009.

---

continue to have a lesser role than men in most branches of most religions. At the same time, most religious groups include those who work for more inclusive approaches to gender. Similarly, in religions in which homophobia is dominant, there are those working against it. Groups whose leading members excuse war and poverty include people struggling for peace and economic alternatives.

Ironically, we can find a remarkable level of similarity *between* religions when we compare their internal conflicts. It seems that when conflict occurs within religions, those groups and views that reflect society's priorities generally have an advantage. To understand this more fully, we need to look at how those with social, political and economic power effectively encourage the most socially conservative aspects of religions while weakening their radicalism.

In most societies, the powerful react to challenging ideas by suppressing them forcibly, by demonizing them, by mocking them or simply by ignoring them. When radical ideas become more influential, the powerful may attempt to compromise or neutralize the opposition by accepting – either nominally or genuinely – some of its ideas.

Many countries have recently experienced this situation with regard to environmental issues. These were once the concerns of a small minority, but it is now common for governments of all persuasions, as well as transnational corporations and the media, to speak of the need to tackle climate change. Some are undoubtedly less serious and genuine than others, but the fact that they feel the need to speak of it at all shows the success of the environmental movement in shifting public opinion and priorities.

Similar dynamics operate with religion. An excellent case-study is provided by the transformation of Christianity from a radical religion on the margins of society to an international power. Christianity developed in the first century CE in Palestine and southeast Europe. In its early years, Christians acted on a socially radical view of humanity that questioned common views of status and wealth. Paul of Tarsus, one of the first Christian leaders, wrote that:

> There is no longer Jew or Greek, there is no longer slave or free, there is no longer male or female, for you are all one in Christ Jesus.[6]

However, as Christianity spread, this radicalism began to soften. Christians became more accepting of prevailing social norms. However, most still refused to join the army or recognize the Roman Emperor as Lord, on the grounds that only Christ was Lord. By the early fourth century, about a tenth of the population of the Roman Empire was Christian.

The turning point came in 313 when the Emperor Constantine granted freedom from persecution to Christians. This was followed by increased imperial backing for Christianity, with major funding for new church buildings and Christian clergy exempted from taxation. Christianity soon became the official religion of the Empire.

Understandably, many Christian leaders thought that God had delivered their people from persecution. However, the Church was flooded with new converts, many motivated by the social and political approval which Christian identity now brought. This aided the abandonment of radicalism necessary for imperial endorsement. By 416, non-Christians had been banned from joining the civil service or the army.

Rather than suppressing Christianity with overt violence, the Roman Empire had domesticated it. A vocal challenge from a religious minority was almost entirely removed and the Christian God was soon being called on to condone imperial structures, policies and wars. The writer Stuart Murray calls this change 'the Christendom shift'.[7] The term 'Christendom' refers to structures and cultures in which Christianity is politically and socially dominant, with the Church giving spiritual sanction to the state and the state providing military and political authority to the Church. In much of Europe, Christendom survived in one form or another until well into the 20th century. Many other governments have taken a domesticating approach to religious movements, although they often do so less visibly or on a smaller scale. The Chinese authorities, for example, have responded to the recent revival of Confucian ideas in China by associating their policies with traditional Confucian values such as harmony.

One of the effects of Christendom was that being Christian became at least as much a matter of birth or culture as of religious choice. The same can of course be said for many other religions, especially when they become the dominant faith within a given country or society and many people belong out of habit rather than conviction. When this happens, those elements of the religion that go against wider social hegemony tend to be downplayed.

For example, the scholar Eleanor Nesbitt carried out research in Coventry, a British city with a large number of Sikhs. The majority of Coventry Sikhs were born in Britain of Punjabi descent. Most of the young Sikhs interviewed equated being Sikh with being Punjabi and used the terms interchangeably. Many did not realize that in the Punjab itself only about two-thirds of the population is Sikh. The founder of Sikhism, Guru Nanak, criticized the Indian caste system, encouraging his followers to: 'Call everyone noble; none is lowborn'.[8] However, as Nesbitt points out, it is common for British Sikhs to check on the caste background of potential partners for their sons and daughters.[9] A confusion of culture with religion can easily lead to a religion's radical teachings being sidelined when they conflict with cultural norms.

## Unholy alliances

When religious leaders become part of the social order, they tend to be less interested in changing social structures and focus instead on changing individual lives. In this context, structural immoralities such

---

### Pro-Palestinian Zionism

'I consider myself a Pro-Palestinian Zionist. To some people this is an oxymoron as the word Zionism in today's language doesn't seem. to many to make allowances for my belief in Palestinian rights. However, to me, this idea works perfectly, as a strong belief in the need for the Jews to have a homeland must bring with it an understanding of the need of the Palestinians to have one too. People who call themselves Zionist but don't acknowledge the Palestinian state or call themselves Pro-Palestinian without recognizing Israel fail the cause they intend to champion as peaceful co-existence and equality is the only way for a long term realization of either cause. To me, it is the concept of an anti-Palestinian Zionist that is actually the oxymoron.' ■
Louise Mitchell, Britain

Louise Mitchell, correspondence with the author, 2 September 2009.

---

as imbalances of wealth and abuses of power are overlooked while more personal immoralities attract attention. A focus on private morality is far less threatening to those with power than a broader ethical concern that includes political and economic justice.

Such a focus has itself often been used as an excuse for oppression, with many religious leaders, particularly in Abrahamic religions, using their religion to justify homophobia. In recent years, Christians, Muslims and Jews who are themselves gay, lesbian, bisexual or transgendered have spoken up strongly against this linking of religion with persecution. They insist that equality and freedom from prejudice are issues of justice and that their faith communities should be supporting them. Paradoxically, the religious emphasis on personal morality is encouraged by secularists who argue that religion should be confined to 'private life'. However, an excessive emphasis on sexuality and personal relationships can easily go along with a willingness to ignore, or even uphold, political oppression.

This is especially so when those with political power ally themselves with the most socially conservative elements of a religion. In the US from the 1980s, the right-wing Republican Party targeted the country's large number of Evangelical Christians by backing their concerns on issues such as abortion and marriage. It is questionable how much these issues mattered to most Republican politicians themselves. However, Evangelicals moved from a fairly mixed political position to being a solid Republican supporter-base. A minority of Evangelicals have suggested that this alliance has meant they have effectively ignored the Republicans' approach to issues such as poverty, war and the environment.

In Saudi Arabia, the state bases its approach on the teachings of Muhammad ibn Abd al-Wahhab (1703-92), who believed in strict adherence to what he regarded as the lifestyle and methods of the early Muslim community. In practice, the Saudi regime uses extreme laws and punishments to control precise details of personal relationships and everyday life. Not only are these controls contrary to the far more compassionate approach of early Muslims, but they are not in reality applied to the ruling élite, who are famed for their lavish lifestyles. The Saudi regime insists that the country is governed by the Qur'an, a claim that angers many Muslims who believe that the inequality and oppression of Saudi society are contrary to the most basic Qur'anic principles.

By its claims about the Qur'an, the Saudi regime is acting in a long tradition of identifying a state so closely with a religion that it confuses religious loyalty with state loyalty. Such attitudes can also be found in far more democratic societies. In New Zealand/Aotearoa, the conservative Christian bishop Brian Tamaki accused the government of 'some type of treason' in 2007 when it promoted a declaration stating that the country had 'no state religion'.[10] For a more extreme example, consider the words of the influential US Christian fundamentalist Jerry Falwell in 1980:

> *It is God Almighty who has made and preserved us a nation... It is only as we abide by those laws established by our Creator that he will continue to bless us... I am positive in my belief regarding the Constitution that God led in the development of that document, and as a result, we here in America have enjoyed 204 years of unparalleled freedom.*[11]

Political leaders who identify themselves with a religion frequently imply that members of that religion have an obligation to support them. When under threat in 2001, the Taliban regime in Afghanistan called on

Muslims worldwide to defend them, although the vast majority of Muslims reject their extremism and brutality. In Sri Lanka, Buddhism became a symbol of national identity in the country's struggle for independence and now serves as a unifying force for those opposed to the (mostly Hindu) Tamils fighting for a separate state.

Such a process can be exacerbated when religious groups feel under threat, and loyalty to the religious group becomes more important than faithfulness to its teachings. A number of European Christians fear the loss of Europe's 'Christian heritage' and so back very right-wing parties willing to give Christians privileges over the rest of society. Indian nationalists argue that their country is Hindu and that Hindus should not be expected to support equal rights for Muslims or Christians. Significant numbers of Muslims speak of loyalty to 'Islam' in a vague and defensive way that in effect sometimes means loyalty to the governments of Muslim-majority countries.

However, when it comes to fusing membership of a religion with loyalty to a state, few have gone so far as the minority of right-wing Jews who are committed to the expansion of Israel at virtually any cost. They are backed by Christian fundamentalists whose devotion is just as extreme.

Until the 20th century only a minority of Jews believed in creating a Jewish homeland in the Middle East. Zionism was originally a secular movement whose supporters felt that the Jewish people must save themselves from centuries of persecution rather than waiting for God. A range of political changes in the first half of the 20th century made the State of Israel a reality. In a very short space of time, belief in a literal homeland became dominant within the main branches of Judaism in most parts of the world. Antisemitism had reached its terrible zenith in the murder of six million Jews by the Nazis; Jewish people were naturally in fear not only of persecution but of annihilation. Their own homeland seemed to provide an answer. Once established, it was much easier to believe in a homeland that existed than in one that seemed like an unrealistic dream.

Since 1967, Israeli forces have occupied the West Bank and Gaza Strip, where colonial settlers have sought to expand Israeli land and Palestinian civilians are denied many of their human rights. Given the number of people opposed to the existence of Israel, it is perhaps no surprise that Jewish fear of annihilation developed into fear of the destruction of Israel. However, this has encouraged a tendency in some circles to overlook human rights abuses committed by Israeli forces or settlers when they are seen – inaccurately – as the only alternative to defeat for Israel.

Many Jews, including many Zionists, oppose occupation and the denial of human rights, insisting that Zionism is about a Jewish homeland, not about forcing others from their homes. Debates around this situation are complicated by the frequent use of the word 'Zionist' to describe a belief in Israeli expansion, when others argue that it refers only to a belief in Israel's continued existence.

Only a small minority of Jews continue to oppose the existence of the State of Israel. At the other extreme are those who defend the extension of Israel at virtually any cost. Such views are often framed in religious language. Rabbi Zvi Yehuda Kook said that 'every soldier added to the army of Israel constitutes another spiritual stage, literally; another stage in the process of redemption'. Karen Armstrong argues that they seem to have replaced faithfulness to God with devotion to the Land.[12]

While most Jews believe strongly that Israel should exist, many oppose continued expansion and criticize the persecution of Palestinians. They point out that the Jewish faith began as a religion of slaves and quote God's calls for compassion, mentioned repeatedly in the Torah:

> *You shall not wrong or oppress a resident alien, for you were aliens in the land of Egypt. You shall not abuse any widow or orphan. If you do abuse them, when they cry out to me, I will surely heed their cry; my wrath will burn.*[13]

In a fascinating twist on the link between religion and power, Israeli authorities and settlers are defended by fundamentalist Protestant Christians who believe that Christ will not return to Earth until the land of Israel is fully restored to the Jews. Christian Zionists can be as hardline as any Jewish group in their defense of Israel. This is very important politically, as such Christians have significant lobbying power in the US and, allied with those who see strategic and military reasons for a US ally in the Middle East, they have played an important part in sustaining the country's alliance with Israel.

This is a striking example of the way in which reactionary movements in various religions help each other to maintain injustice. It is not unusual. In several countries, groups from different religions have united to campaign against equal rights for gay, lesbian and bisexual people.

This is one reason why we need always to remember the dynamics *within* religious groups when considering the relationship between religion and oppression. Within any one religion, certain people and ideas may be reinforcing hegemony, while others may be going against it. Those religious elements that sustain the social order generally have the backing of people with power and much easier access to forms of mass communication, whether the pulpits of medieval Europe or the televisions of today. Further, they are often fueled by the success of socially conservative movements in religions other than their own.

In contrast, the situation is much harder for religious movements that go against society's priorities, oppose the powerful or disrupt understandings within their own religion. It is now time to look at why many such movements are surprisingly successful, despite the cards being stacked against them.

**1** Cecil Frances Alexander, 'All Things Bright and Beautiful' in *Hymns Ancient and Modern* (Church of England, 1875) edited by William Henry Monk. **2** Jon Weiner, 'Christopher Hitchens: Religion poisons everything' in *Truthdig,* 6 June 2007. **3** Karl Marx, 'A Contribution to the Critique of Hegel's Philosophy of Right' [1843] in *Marx: Early Political Writings* (Cambridge University Press, 1994). **4** *Daily Star,* London, 16 October 2008. **5** Leila Gal Berner, 'Hearing Hannah's voice: the Jewish feminist challenge and ritual innovation' in *Daughters of Abraham,* edited by Yvonne Yazbeck Haddad and John L Esposito (University Press of Florida, 2001). **6** Galatians 3, 28, *The Bible, New Revised Standard Version* (Cambridge University Press, 1993). **7** Stuart Murray, *Post-Christendom* (Paternoster Press, 2004). **8** Nicky-Guninnder Kaur Singh, *The Name of my Beloved: Verses of the Sikh Gurus* (Harper San Francisco, 1996). **9** Eleanor Nesbitt, *Sikhism* (Oxford University Press, 2005). **10** Simon Collins, 'Denying state religion like treason, says Brian Tamaki' in *New Zealand Herald,* 17 February 2007. **11** Cited by David Domke and Kevin Coe, *The God Strategy: How religion became a political weapon in America* (Oxford University Press, 2008). **12** Karen Armstrong, *The Battle for God* (Harper Collins, 2000). **13** Exodus 22, 21-24, *The Bible, New Revised Standard Version* (Cambridge University Press, 1993).

# 5 Resistance and liberation

**For every example of a link between religion and oppression, there is a link between religion and liberation. Throughout the world and across the centuries, religion has inspired people to stand up against injustice, to side with the oppressed and to struggle for a better world.**

MANY OF THESE examples are not as well known as the links between religion and oppression, but they are not difficult to find. As recently as 2007, Buddhist monks in Burma gained the world's attention by marching without violence against their country's brutal despotism. Going back to the 16th century, we can find Anabaptist Christians in central Europe risking their lives by defying political and religious leaders and sharing their goods in common. Looking back even further, we find the 10th-century Muslim mystic al-Husayn ibn Mansur al-Hallaj preaching in Baghdad that all can seek God for themselves and appeal to divine justice. We can even go as far back as the fifth century BCE, when the Chinese religious thinker Mozi challenged rulers and governments to adopt ethics of nonviolence and equality.

But what is the connection between these people's religion and their resistance to power? A cynic might say that their religion really had nothing to do with their political action, that they would have done it anyway. So does religion really have the power to provoke effective struggles for justice?

Can religion be a force for social change? Without getting hung up on definitions, this means religious groups and their adherents speaking of justice and liberation in ways that involve an active religious commitment to work for a better world in the here and now.

**Against the grain**

Beliefs and theology can be extremely important in determining political behavior, but social and economic circumstances can be equally vital, often strengthening or weakening different interpretations of religion.

This is, of course, only a variation on the notion that people are more likely to resist a political decision if they feel affected by it. When the UK joined the US in invading Iraq in 2003, British Muslims found common cause with many peace activists of other religions and of none. There was a strong feeling that the 'war on terror' announced by the US and British governments was to some extent really a war on Islam. Muslim communities and organizations used their own structures to promote campaigns against the invasion and to mobilize their members to participate in them. Polls repeatedly showed that the majority of the British population opposed the war and many churches and other faith groups joined in the opposition. However, most churches came nowhere near to the level of involvement of the Muslim community. The difference can be attributed in some measure to a variation in how much each group felt directly affected by the political decision in question.

However, not all religious groups actively oppose power when they feel under attack from it. Some respond to persecution by trying to withdraw from political life, hoping they will not be targeted if they are as quiet as possible. Others are so keen not to be seen as a threat that they may abandon their distinctive behavior or lifestyles. Even amongst those who do resist power, there may be more of a concern with preserving the group's identity than with securing justice.

We can see all these patterns of behavior in France when we consider the government's ban on religious dress in schools and certain other public situations. Some religious individuals have responded by abandoning distinctive dress or wearing it only in private. Others who have fought the ban have focused on their own religion's identity. However, the most striking campaigns for freedom of dress have united people of different faiths in campaigning for general rights to freedom of expression.

Many protests triggered by social and economic conditions are reported in terms of their religious elements. Civil rights struggles in Northern Ireland in the 1960s were about political and economic equality, but they quickly took on a religious dimension, with elements of the majority Protestant population reacting against Catholics' calls for change. While the causes of the conflict were primarily economic, the use of religious labels provided a simpler way of looking at the situation. This in turn fueled the conflict by encouraging people to take sides based on religious identity. Palestinian opposition to Israeli occupation frequently invokes religious language and many Palestinian activists are strengthened by their Muslim (or sometimes Christian) faith. This does not mean that it is not real political and economic oppression that they are resisting. As the scholar Beverley Milton-Edwards puts it:

> *Most politically active Muslims are spurred on by issues of justice, rights, and the place of faith in politics and society, including economic status, in the modern world. Muslim communities are inextricably tied into the modern global tempo and are, by virtue of their human condition, moved to react to it. If the majority of Muslim populations live in countries characterized by economic crisis, poverty... and authoritarian governance, it is natural to find opposition and protest associated with a demand for change.*[1]

The majority of Muslim protests in the world are against Muslim governments. Similarly, much Christian protest is found in Christian-majority countries. In many cases in which religious people oppose the powerful, they are opposing members of their own religion. Thus, religious calls for social and political change are not simply about a religion's own position in society. Instead, there are other factors at play.

**A different loyalty**

Here we come to a crucial but often overlooked point about religion. Religion generally involves a loyalty to the divine or transcendent, whether in the form of a personal God or gods or an impersonal reality. For most committed religious people, this means that the divine has the first call on their allegiance – more than state, nation, army, political party or human rulers. It is therefore no surprise that many monarchs and governments have been keen to identify themselves

---

### Buddhism and politics

'Those who think that Buddhism is interested only in lofty ideals, high moral and philosophical thought, and that it ignores the social and economic welfare of people, are wrong... Buddhism aims at creating a society where the ruinous struggle for power is renounced; where calm and peace prevail away from conquest and defeat; where the persecution of the innocent is vehemently denounced; where one who conquers oneself is more respected than those who conquer millions by military and economic warfare; where hatred is conquered by kindness, and evil by goodness; where enmity, jealousy, ill-will and greed do not infect men's minds; where compassion is the driving force of action; where all, including the least of living things, are treated with fairness, consideration and love; where life in peace and harmony, in a world of material contentment, is directed towards the highest and noblest aim, the realization of the Ultimate Truth, Nirvana.' ■
Walpola Rahula

Walpola Rahula, 'The Social Teachings of the Buddha' in *The Path of Compassion*, edited by Fred Eppsteiner (Parallax Press, 1988).

with divine will. When Japanese emperors claimed divine anointing, they suggested that to rebel against them was to undermine the ordering of the world. Conservative religious leaders in Iran imply that to be disloyal to the regime is to oppose the God who upholds it. When Israeli settlers insist that their actions are necessarily blessed by God, they put criticism of a human movement on a level with blasphemy.

Such people can hardly claim that their monarchs, governments, armies and systems are entitled to *more* loyalty than the divine. The trick of identifying the divine with authority and injustice is a well-developed one, for once the link between them is broken, faithful religious adherents find that no human authority can ever demand their total loyalty.

In the Abrahamic traditions in particular, mystical movements that have spoken of the individual's direct connection with God have often been suppressed by political and religious leaders who wish their own views and priorities to be identified with God's will. Mysticism is sometimes associated with a purely personal process, a rather selfish withdrawal from the affairs of the world. But the root of mysticism is a conviction that each person can find the divine for him/herself by turning inward, a truly revolutionary notion. Mysticism tends to subvert social expectations – a number of the world's most prominent mystics have been women. They include the Muslim Rabia al-Adawiyya (713-801), the Hindu Mirabai (1498-1546) and the Christian Teresa of Avila (1515-82), all of whom had to contend with hostility from those who objected to women taking on the lifestyles that they chose.

At its best, mystical practice and experience equip the mystic for engagement with the world. These connections have been made by political radicals from many religious traditions. The 17th-century English writer Gerard Winstanley (1609-76), who founded a radical Christian movement known as the Diggers, based his appeals for equality and common ownership on the principle that God's spirit dwelt in all people and that everyone has God 'to his Teacher and Ruler within himself'.[2] Gandhi linked individual spirituality to political liberation through his concept of Truth. As the writer Rex Ambler puts it, he 'saw the universal availability of Truth as a source of personal liberation and independence, which would in turn provide the basis of genuine liberation and independence for India'.[3] In recent decades, the movement known as 'socially engaged Buddhism' has emphasized the political outworking of the Buddha's teachings, without neglecting the inward dimensions. As the British Buddhist Christopher Titmuss puts it:

> *There is a greater sense coming about that the inner and outer are not really separate. I feel this awareness is very, very important. More and more meditators are becoming involved in major issues affecting this planet... Equally important, people who are already involved in direct action are coming to retreats and therefore are giving consideration to their inner selves as well as what is happening out in the world... Both are giving more and more support to each other and the genuine liberation of both people and planet.[4]*

Quakerism is another movement that has developed a deep understanding of the relationship between inner and outer. The Quakers, known more formally as the Religious Society of Friends, are founded on a distinctive interpretation of Christianity. Believing that everyone can find God inwardly, they have developed the concept of Testimony, which refers to outward actions performed as a witness to their inward experience of God. Inward experience convinces them that God can turn the world towards nonviolence, leading to a testimony to campaign for peace. After experiencing the divine as a God who values and loves the world, they can testify to this by living environmentally sustainable lifestyles.

This is not to deny that mystical movements have at times taken very individualistic approaches and focused excessively on personal experience. But such criticisms have often been overstated. Sufism, a longstanding and wide-ranging mystical movement within Islam, is sometimes accused of esotericism, but such a view is dependent on a rather selective reading of its history. Sufis have also been revolutionary, frequently suggesting that the power of God accessible in people's hearts is greater than the transient power of political authorities.

## Taking sides

The difficulties faced by religious adherents hoping to challenge power and oppression were highlighted with precision in South Africa during the years of apartheid. A group of Christian activists and theologians produced a statement on the country's situation in 1985, known as the Kairos Document. They pointed out three types of theology then present amongst South African Christians. These three approaches undoubtedly have their parallels in other contexts and countries and within other religions.

The first type they called 'state theology'. This was the official view of certain churches that apartheid was sanctioned by God. However, this was not the dominant view even amongst white church leaders. Rather, most church leaders in South Africa subscribed to what the Kairos writers called 'church theology'. This involved criticism of apartheid and talk of the need for reconciliation and justice. However, the Kairos Document pointed out the dangers of this approach:

*There are conflicts where one side is a fully
armed and violent oppressor while the other
side is defenseless and oppressed. There are
conflicts that can only be described as the
struggle between justice and injustice, good and
evil, God and the devil. To speak of reconciling
these two is not only a mistaken application
of the Christian idea of reconciliation, it is a
total betrayal of all that Christian faith has
ever meant... We are supposed to do away
with evil, injustice, oppression and sin – not
come to terms with it.[5]*

Rejecting both 'state theology' and 'church theology',
the Kairos writers called instead for 'prophetic
theology', which means recognizing that God is
not neutral, but sides with the oppressed and that
Christians are called to do the same. A similar point
had been made the previous year by the founders of
the Call of Islam, a left-wing South African movement
that urged Muslims to work alongside others in the
struggle against apartheid.

The point that they were both making is very
important and applies to many other contexts,
countries and religions. Religious groups are unlikely
to challenge a political system to any significant extent
if they do not make a deliberate choice to take a stand
against it. Social acceptability, political power and
cultural norms all work together to make acceptance
– or at least tolerance – of the current system into
the default position. South African campaigners were
keen to point out that to remain neutral in a situation
of oppression is to tolerate the status quo and thus, in
effect, to side with the oppressor.

Both Kairos and the Call of Islam were influenced
by the movement known as liberation theology. In
its broadest sense, liberation theology is a term that
can be used for any way of looking at religion that

emphasizes the need for social and political liberation. Used more precisely, it refers to a movement that developed amongst Roman Catholics in Latin America in the late 1960s and early 1970s, the principles of which have since been applied in other parts of the world and by members of other religious groups.

The key point to understanding liberation theology is that it starts from the perspective and experience of the poor, oppressed and marginalized. Thus it takes as its starting-point the notion that God sides with the victims of injustice. Liberation theologians typically acknowledge that they are very influenced by their own background and context but are keen to emphasize that this applies to all other theologians and indeed to all people considering any issue whatsoever. They suggest that the façade of disinterested study masks the reality that most mainstream theologians in the West are producing theology that ultimately benefits the rich and the powerful by treating political issues as of secondary interest.

Liberation theologians emphasize that critical reflection on society and religion can be undertaken by anyone and is an important task of grassroots Christians. Latin America saw the emergence of 'base communities', small groups of Christians engaging in theology from their own experience and perspective. For these communities, theology is not simply an academic discipline unrelated to other forms of study or to everyday life. It is critical reflection on practice. That is to say that practice, action and 'real life' are the starting point. Theology is about responding to them. As the influential Peruvian liberation theologian Gustavo Gutierrez put it in the early days of the movement, theological reflection is about 'criticism of society and the Church... worked out in the light of the Word [of God] accepted in faith and inspired by a practical purpose'.[6]

Liberation theology soon spread beyond Roman

Catholicism and beyond Latin America. It has influenced Christians fighting injustice in every continent, from black theologians in the United States to impoverished Protestants in South Korea. It has contributed to the shaping of feminist theology and to the theological reflections of gay, lesbian and bisexual Christians struggling against prejudice and persecution. Liberation theologians' commitment to starting from their own contexts means that this is not a theory that can be exported wholesale from one society to the next but must be built up from the grassroots on each occasion.

Movements outside Christianity have developed approaches with similarities to liberation theology. Some have taken on board individual points without always using the language of liberation. Others, including Jewish, Muslim and Hindu theologians, have talked explicitly about developing a liberation theology within their own faith.

The Muslim liberation theologian Farid Esack suggests that God is more concerned with upholding justice than with religious labels, quoting the Qur'an in support of this view:

> *It is not righteousness that ye turn your faces towards East or West; but it is righteousness to believe in Allah... to spend of your substance, out of love for Him, for your kin, for orphans, for the needy, for the wayfarer, for those who ask, and for the ransom of slaves; to be steadfast in prayer, and practice regular charity; to fulfill the contracts which ye have made... Such are the people of truth, the God-fearing.*[7]

In the light of such texts, Esack argues that alliances with non-Muslims in struggles against injustice are not a denial of Islam but a natural outworking of it. He calls for 'interreligious solidarity against oppression'. He also points out that politically conservative religious adherents often work willingly with secular authorities, and indeed with other faith groups, when it suits their agenda. Writing in the context of South Africa, he criticizes 'Muslims and Christians who opposed interfaith solidarity against apartheid [but] worked hand in hand... to oppose pornography'.[8]

Similarly, both secular and religious activists have recognized the need to work with each other in struggles against injustice. The human rights campaigner Peter Tatchell says: 'Although I am an atheist and reject religious superstitions, I work with and support the many people of faith who are campaigning against oppression'.[9]

For some, solidarity implies not only a willingness to put aside differences for the sake of a shared aim, but an openness to being influenced by the teachings of other religions and worldviews. Gandhi, for example, was keen to learn from the insights of both Islam and Christianity, as well as his own faith of Hinduism. He found that, in many ways, Hindus, Muslims and Christians who shared a radical approach to faith and life had more in common with each other than with members of their own religions who were prepared to support oppressive power and to put loyalty to their own religious group ahead of the need for justice.

## Grassroots religion

Movements such as liberation theology and socially engaged Buddhism show that meaningful religious thinking can develop at a grassroots level. This is not always a message that religious leaders want to hear.

This is not to say that religious leaders are concerned only with their own power or position; many are undoubtedly committed and compassionate. However, they often have an understandable desire to preserve social respect for their religion and to avoid damaging disputes amongst its followers. Furthermore, in many religions, leaders are likely to be drawn from the more affluent levels of society. These factors combine to encourage a tendency towards social conservatism amongst religious leaders that grassroots adherents may not share.

Some religions are far more hierarchical than others and such hierarchy may well contribute towards restricting the growth of new approaches or alternative views. However, it would be a mistake to think that hierarchy necessarily goes along with conservatism. For example, it is often mistakenly thought (by non-Catholics) that Roman Catholics believe the Pope – the head of their Church – to be infallible. In reality, Roman Catholic teaching makes

---

## Love, religion and human rights

'The motive of my human rights campaigning is love. I love people. I love justice. I love peace. I love life. I don't like seeing other people suffer. I think to myself: since I wouldn't want my family or friends to suffer, why should I tolerate the suffering of other people's family or friends?

'If we all had love for the wider human family and a zero tolerance of suffering, most of the world's great injustices, like tyranny and hunger, would soon be solved. These values and ideals are shared by many people with faith and without faith. Despite our different belief systems, we can and should work together to solve the great wrongs that beset humanity.

'Working together may sometimes involve compromises for the sake of a greater cause. Several of my campaigns in support of the struggle for democracy and human rights in Zimbabwe have involved working with Christians who are quite homophobic and misogynistic. But as a result of my solidarity as an openly gay man, more than a few of them have changed their harsh attitudes towards LGBT people.

'The way I see it, a different, better world is possible – but we don't need religion to make it happen. What we need is love and people of goodwill who are willing to turn that love into political action for human freedom and liberation.' ∎

Peter Tatchell, human rights campaigner

Peter Tatchell, correspondence with the author, 25 August 2009.

clear that this infallibility applies only when the Pope speaks *ex cathedra* ('from the throne'). This happens on only very rare occasions. Nonetheless, the very hierarchical nature of the Catholic Church can encourage conformity to the leadership's approach and make it harder to promote contrary views. At the same time, this has not stopped the development of radical movements amongst grassroots Catholics which have endorsed socialism, pacifism, feminism and gay rights campaigns.

The ability of grassroots religious adherents to explore a range of views and ideas has been sharply increased in recent years by the globalization of communication. The invention of the internet, like the invention of the printing press half a millennium earlier, is a challenge to every authority – whether political, religious or scientific – that aims to keep control of knowledge and proscribe what should be believed. It allows many people to encounter far more traditions and perspectives than was previously possible. It provides the opportunity to share thoughts and ideas with people of similar or differing views who may live halfway around the globe. As the researcher Brenda E Brasher puts it:

> *The capacity of the internet to minimize human differences is interpreted by some religious leaders as posing an unacceptable challenge to the particularistic worldview their tradition espouses... Other authoritarian religious leaders worry less about what else is in cyberspace, and instead relish the internet as a global space that can be used to convey rigidly controlled messages into the home of every online follower they can attract... How successfully religious authority can be wielded on the internet is another matter. Designed to be an open, participatory medium, the internet generates*

*a public space where it is easy for people to bypass hierarchies, religious or otherwise.*[10]

This is not to deny that the internet itself has created a new form of inequality: between those who have access to it and those who do not. However, the spread of ideas that it generates is likely to have a bigger impact than we can yet fully understand. By facilitating grassroots communication and challenging authority, it has weakened the power of religious leaders and fueled the growth of grassroots movements tackling theological and ethical questions for themselves.

### Speaking up, religiously

Grassroots religious movements emphasize that their approach does not mean simplistic theory, as has sometimes been suggested. Indeed, the writers of the Kairos Document suggested that it was a lack of social, political and theological analysis that led to the shallowness of 'church theology'.

Instead, activists in many religions have developed sophisticated theological understandings. Approaching theology from the perspectives of the marginalized frequently involves a struggle to overcome the influence that centuries of compromise with power have exerted over interpretation. Politically progressive religious scholars and activists use familiar words and phrases in unfamiliar ways. They often insist that they are simply returning to earlier and more authentic ways of using such language.

Mohandas Gandhi, when struggling against British imperial rule in India, made great use of the Hindu concept of *ahimsa*, meaning nonviolence or non-injury. This had been important in India for at least 3,000 years and used by people with a variety of emphases, including promoting personal peace, unity between warring groups and opposition to meat-eating. For Gandhi, it involved a firm commitment to resist the violence of oppression without using violence in response. Those who said that this was changing the meaning of the word could be reminded that it had been used in many and varied ways throughout history. Gandhi and his supporters were keen to make *ahimsa* more meaningful, not less.

Similarly, Muslim feminists have in recent years promoted the concept of 'gender jihad'. The word 'jihad' is often mistakenly translated (usually by non-Muslims) as 'holy war'. A more accurate translation is 'struggle'. This includes both internal struggles to live a godly and selfless life and external struggles for justice. By using this word while speaking of the need for gender equality, Muslim feminists are reminding their listeners that they regard their cause as godly and as a natural consequence of a Qur'anic worldview. At the same time, they are catching their attention by using words in an unusual way.

Feminists of several faiths have looked at their own scriptures and traditions and found them to be more progressive and inclusive than many of the common practices found in their religions would suggest. As the Hindu feminist Lina Gupta puts it:

*Hinduism is not inherently patriarchal; the equal importance of the gods and goddesses in the pantheon would seem to support this. But despite the quality and importance of the goddesses found in various scriptures, traditional Hindu life by and large has remained patriarchal... It seems to me that patriarchal understanding has appropriated the goddesses and the feminine aspects of the Ultimate Reality at the heart of Hinduism in ways that sanction the unequal treatment of men and women.*[11]

A rediscovery of the role of women in scriptures has been a feature of feminist movements in a number of other religions; for example, Christian feminists have pointed out the centrality of Jesus' female disciples in the New Testament. There are countless more instances of people reading their traditions anew in the light of their own social and political circumstances. Jews have been inspired to resist oppression by the biblical story of the Exodus, through which God leads slaves to their freedom. Zoroastrians have reaffirmed their traditional appreciation of the Earth by committing themselves to tackling climate change. Hindus have regarded 'untouchability' as an aberration of their religion rather than a component of it. Muslims have reread the Qur'an's comments on the People of God as relating to all who struggle for justice. Maori people have drawn on their indigenous traditions of peace and applied them to contemporary situations. Sikhs have pointed out the political implications of their traditional duty of hospitality.

Of course, those who take these approaches generally cause conflict with more mainstream and socially acceptable members of their own religions. But people engaged in social, political and economic struggles tend to see spiritual conflict not as a dispute between one religion and another but between the oppressor and the oppressed, the powerful and the powerless, the rich and the rest, or those who benefit from a system and those who do not.

Such an approach is far from the cautious neutrality of many religious leaders. Indeed, it is the insistence of religious activists on taking sides that often angers more conservative adherents of their religion. Activists continue to point out that political neutrality is not a real option. As the South African Christian Desmond Tutu puts it: 'If an elephant has its foot on the tail of a mouse and you say that you are neutral, the mouse will not appreciate your neutrality'.

**1** Beverley Milton-Edwards, *Islam and Politics in the Contemporary World* (Polity Press, 2004). **2** Gerard Winstanley, 'The True Levellers' Standard Advanced' [1649] in *Radical Christian Writings: A Reader*, edited by Andrew Bradstock and Christopher Rowland (Blackwell Publishers, 2002). **3** Rex Ambler, 'Gandhi's Concept of Truth' in *Gandhi's Significance for Today*, edited by John Hick and Lamont Hempel (Macmillan, 1989). **4** Christopher Titmuss, 'Interactivity: Sitting for peace and standing for Parliament' in *The Path of Compassion*, edited by Fred Eppsteiner (Parallax Press, 1988). **5** 'The Kairos Document' [1985] in *Radical Christian Writings: A Reader*, edited by Andrew Bradstock and Christopher Rowland (Blackwell Publishers, 2002). **6** Gustavo Gutierrez, *A Theology of Liberation* (Orbis Books, 1973). **7** *The Qur'an*, 2,177, translated by Abdullah Yusuf Ali (Wordsworth Editions, 2000). **8** Farid Esack, *Qur'an, Liberation and Pluralism* (Oneworld Publications, 1997). **9** Peter Tatchell, correspondence with the author, 25 August 2009. **10** Brenda E Brasher, *Give Me That Online Religion* (Rutgers University Press, 2004). **11** Lina Gupta, 'Kali, the Savior' in *Religion and Social Transformations*, edited by David Herbert (Open University, 2001).

# 6 An elusive freedom

**Religious liberty is a vital aspect of human rights, yet it is restricted to varying degrees in much of the world. Even in relatively democratic countries, influential religious groups lobby to restrict the freedoms of others. Despite this, the globalization of communication is allowing more people than ever before to explore a diversity of religions and make independent choices.**

FREEDOM OF RELIGION is not a new idea. In medieval Spain, the system known as the Conviviencia allowed Christians, Muslims and Jews to flourish side by side, before the practice was brought to an end by a hardline Christian government in 1492. Many modern human rights movements have their origins in campaigns for the rights of religious minorities.

The principle of religious liberty is enshrined in Article 18 of the Universal Declaration of Human Rights, agreed by the United Nations in 1948:

*Everyone has the right to freedom of thought, conscience and religion; this right includes freedom to change his religion or belief, and freedom, either alone or in community with others and in public or private, to manifest his religion or belief in teaching, practice, worship and observance.*

In reality, however, freedom of religion is complex, controversial and elusive. For many of the world's people, it is simply not a reality. For others, their liberty is limited, less than the liberty accorded to other groups or dependent on unreasonable conditions. Abuses of religious freedom in 2009 included the arrest of Falun Gong practitioners in China, harassment of Baptists in Turkmenistan and renewed assaults on the freedom to wear forms of Muslim dress in France. These are but three examples of the hundreds that could be cited.

There are several countries in which one religion or worldview is dominant to the point that the followers of other faiths are persecuted. In North Korea, all religion is suppressed, although many have suggested that the state ideology of Juche is effectively a religion in itself. The four Christian churches in the capital Pyongyang appear to be designed to give tourists an impression of liberty; human rights groups report never seeing a Korean enter them.

Regimes that are closely linked with a particular religion do not usually confine themselves to persecuting alternative religions but are frequently even more active in suppressing alternative interpretations of the dominant religion. Muslims in Saudi Arabia who do not adhere to the regime's narrow interpretation of Islam have seen their writings suppressed and faced imprisonment and torture. The harassment by the Russian authorities of minority Christian groups such as Jehovah's Witnesses and the Salvation Army has been encouraged by some (but not all) senior figures in the Russian Orthodox Church, the country's largest religious grouping.

In several countries, larger religious groups enjoy a fairly high level of liberty while smaller or more controversial groups face persecution. Since the 1990s, the Egyptian government has required its citizens to state their religion on identity documents such as passports, but allowed only Christianity, Islam and Judaism to be listed. The largest religious minority to be affected by this discrimination is the country's several thousand Baha'is, who appear to be making slow progress through legal action despite bans on much of their activity. Several governments require religious groups to be registered, discriminating against those which are not. In 2008, the Macedonian authorities approved a 'Religion Law' which recognized two major faith communities in the country, the Macedonian Orthodox Church and the Islamic Community of Macedonia. The law allowed certain other groups to register to gain official status, but registration has been denied or delayed to sizeable groups such as the Serbian Orthodox Church and the Bektashi Muslims.

The abuse of religious liberty is often complex and not easy to document. It can be difficult to draw comparisons between one country and another. Take for example the differences between the UK and the US. In the UK, the Church of England has official approval, with the monarch as its 'supreme governor' and its bishops able to sit and vote in the House of Lords, the upper house of Parliament. In the US, the constitution guarantees separation of religion and state. However, while the British situation is far from democratic, the influence of church leaders on politics in the country appears to be considerably less than in the US, where presidential candidates go to great lengths to secure religious endorsement. The greater number of committed Christians in the States means that organizations promoting their concerns carry more weight; they also tend to be better organized and financially stronger.

### Choice and conversion

The majority of people live and die in the religion into which they were born. This applies even to the majority of deeply committed religious adherents; it is not simply due to nominalism. Of course, we are all very much influenced by our background, culture and experiences. They will affect our political views and ethics as much as our choice of religious affiliation.

However, religious movements are fluid entities. Those who stay in the 'same' religion as their parents may well lead it in different directions. Furthermore, the globalization of communication is enabling millions of people to hear about religions and ideas which they would not previously have encountered. Future historians will be able to assess the impact of the internet as we now consider the effects of the invention of the printing press. It is already likely that more people globally belong to a different religion from their parents than has ever been the case before. Brenda E Brasher gives an example of a US woman in her twenties who became interested in Judaism:

> *Ashley chose to begin learning about Judaism by logging on to the internet... The link that intrigued her the most extended an invitation to attend a Cyber-Seder... Traditionally, the seder is a home-based Jewish ceremony... To some, conducting a seder in cyberspace, where people viewed the storytelling in the company of machines rather than one another, was a profound contradiction of the human sociability the seder was dedicated to cultivating. To Ashley, these criticisms were moot. Had there not been a Cyber-Seder, she would have attended no seder at all... Six months after her Cyber-Seder experience, Ashley decided to convert to Judaism.*[1]

For many people conversion brings a sense of fulfillment, as they choose to follow something that truly matters to them. Conversion often affects all aspects of a person's life, including relationships and lifestyle as much as beliefs. The psychologist Kate Loewenthal explains that 'sometimes the convert is helped to see purpose and fulfillment in existing relationships and work, sometimes these may be changed in the light of new values and morality, and sometimes the religious group may encourage or help the development of new relationships'. She emphasizes the need to see conversion in the context of wider personal changes, which 'continue throughout life'.[2]

Conversion, however, is rarely an easy matter. In certain repressive states, converting away from the dominant religion can lead to a denial of human rights or at least a reduction in social status and career prospects. Even in more liberal societies, conversion is often met with family disapproval. Lucy Bushill-Matthews, an English woman who converted to Islam while a student, describes the reaction her decision provoked:

> *I came across several letters of condolence lying around the study, addressed to my parents. 'How terrible for you,' wrote one lady who I knew well. She used to babysit me when I was a child. I thought somebody might have died – until I continued reading. Nobody had died. She was writing about me. I felt incredibly alone.*[3]

Given such difficulties, conversion usually requires very strong convictions. However, in addition to the spiritual and psychological motivations, conversion can also be politically liberating. In recent decades, considerable numbers of Indian Dalits – those outside the caste system, traditionally labeled 'untouchables' – have turned away from Hinduism and converted to Buddhism or Christianity, feeling that this enables them to leave the caste system behind. Similarly, the researcher Kate Zebiri found in her study of British Muslim converts that disillusionment with dominant social and political values is often a factor in triggering interest in Islam.[4]

The political consequences of conversion can also apply to people who significantly alter their understanding of their own religion's teachings. Many Dalits have remained Hindu but embraced understandings of Hinduism that reject the caste system. The British activist Tamsin Omond describes how her commitment to Christianity took a new turn when she was a student:

> *I was brought up as a Christian... In my final year at Cambridge, I shared a house with some people from Plane Stupid who told me about climate change... I read all their stuff and these two worlds really came together for me: the Christian call to stewardship of the Earth and the awful implications of climate change, not only for our way of life now but for the future of humanity, and what it will say about us if we allow it to happen... My environmentalism and my faith are totally connected and intertwined... Either we can realize all the promise of this Earth or we can make it desolate.[5]*

In the light of such examples, it is clear that the positive consequences of conversion – such as personal

---

### Religion and freedom of dress

'I put on my *niqab*, my face veil, each day before I leave the house, without a second thought... I made this choice from my own free will, as did the vast majority of covered women of my generation... Muslim women have been saying for years that the *hijab* et al are not oppressive, that we cover as an act of faith, that this is a bona fide spiritual lifestyle choice. But the debate rages on, ironically, largely to the exclusion of the women who actually do cover their faces...

'All women, covered or not, deserve the opportunity to dress as they see fit, to be educated, to work where they deem appropriate and run their lives in accordance with their principles, as long as these choices do not impinge on others' freedoms... I have been able to study, to work, to establish a writing career and run a magazine business, all while wearing a niqab.' ∎

Na'ima B Robert

Na'ima B Robert, 'Niqabi, Interrupted' in *Times Online*, 26 June 2009.

fulfillment and political commitment – can be just as relevant to those who choose to make a renewed or deeper commitment to the religion in which they grew up. The most vital factor seems to be the element of personal choice and commitment, rather than the move between one religious identity and another.

## Private and public

The range of movements broadly described as 'secularist' have at times played important roles in promoting religious liberty. Secularists have worked to end religious domination of politics and prevent the establishment of any official religion with links to the state. However, the word is now frequently applied to those who want to remove religion from politics altogether. Some who put forward such an argument imply that if religion were kept to 'private life', then we would see an end to religiously based conflict in politics or society. Such an approach is naive. A committed follower of a religion generally seeks to apply his/her religion to the whole of life. It will influence how he/she votes as much as whom he/she marries. This may not be the case with more nominal religion, although as nominal religion is often a reflection of culture, it will also have an effect on politics and ethics. To ask people to take a view on abortion, war or climate change without reference to their religion or worldview is effectively to ask them to abandon their religion or worldview in favor of the prevailing outlook.

The notion of confining religion to private life is really a very new idea. For most of history, religion has been an extremely public matter. It has given a sense of unity to communities under threat, provided myths and rituals to help them understand their communal identity and established a framework for ethical and political decisions. Its effects on such communities may have been negative as often as positive, but the difference is over how religion has been used, rather than the existence of religion itself.

Scholars suggest that prior to the first millennium BCE, religion was an almost entirely public affair. The Axial Age of the eighth to the third centuries BCE led to what Karen Armstrong calls the 'interiorization' of religion.[6] This saw religious teachers in cultures as far apart as India, Greece, China and the Middle East develop understandings of compassion linked to experience of the divine. Following the Axial Age, religion became for many a personal as well as a public matter, but the primary focus of religious activity remained in the public sphere. For many people, the notion that religion should apply only to private life would have made no sense at all. When the Victorian British Prime Minister William Melbourne heard an Evangelical sermon encouraging Christians to apply their ethics to their everyday lives, he expressed his horror that 'religion is allowed to invade *private* life'.[7] His own attempt to contain religion was the opposite approach. He wanted religion to be *exclusively* public, involving ceremonies and teaching that gave endorsement to national structures and priorities, not complex ethical questions for people to make choices about.

However, it is no surprise that some of those who argue for religion to be kept to private life are motivated by a fear of the undemocratic influence that religious groups may exert over politics. Such a fear is very understandable given the number of religious groups that have successfully lobbied for oppressive policies such as the denial of human rights to women and to gay, lesbian and bisexual people. However, attempts to draw a sharp distinction between 'public' politics and 'private' religion have often caused as much conflict as they were intended to prevent. This has been seen in several countries, such as France and Turkey, that have attempted to impose severe restrictions on religious dress in public. The French situation is unusual, as their country's history of democracy since the late 18th century has involved an emphasis on national unity to the point of excluding cultural differences that are thought to undermine equality. While this tradition is deeply ingrained, it is far from being the only basis for campaigns against religious dress. Much of the discussion focuses particularly on Muslim dress and is fueled by assumptions and prejudices that regard Islam as sexist and see the Muslim headscarf, or *hijab*, as a symbol of oppression. But, as the Norwegian human rights commentator Kristine Rodstol puts it, 'If a Muslim woman finds it demeaning to be forced to remove her hijab at school or at work, how does this promote human rights?[8]

The reality is that the overlap between religious dress and cultural dress can lead minorities to feel under attack on racial as well as religious grounds. Rodstol points to Sweden as a country that has achieved more success with separating religion and the state since the Lutheran Church was formally disestablished in 1995. She suggests that Sweden gives 'equal benefit to all religious communities' whereas France seeks to discriminate against them all but ends up marginalizing some more than others.

Another problem with attempts to confine religion to private life involves the issues with which religious groups and their leaders concern themselves. When religious groups become allied with power – or at least comfortable with it – they are more likely to focus on issues of 'personal' morality than on structural and political injustices. The emphasis on 'private life' gives fuel to those elements of religion whose ethical and political outlook focuses disproportionately on issues of sexual morality to the exclusion of any critique of poverty, racism or environmental destruction. Politically progressive elements within religious groups will not be helped by attempts to confine religion to private life.

---

**Evangelicals and public life**

'I am interested and active in politics because I am a Christian, and an Evangelical one at that. Within US political dialogue, if we can call it that, there is much debate about whether or not religion should keep its two cents to itself. Some on the left say, "keep it out of the public square", while others on the right try to bully their way in, like a party they weren't invited to. This all operates under the assumption that there really is some religion-free, neutral space like a "public square".

'I gladly do not identify with either the left or right because for me to be a Christian is to pledge allegiance to only one political party, Christ's kingdom. The Christian church is at its very core political. If I get my ethics from the Sermon on the Mount, then as a Christian I play politics to a radically different drumbeat. Deep within Jesus' sayings, his parables, and his miracles is a world of reversals, subversions, and love where the losers are winners, the mournful rejoice and the wounded are healed. It sides with the weak, the poor, the orphan and the widow. This is how the world looks like right-side up. This is the throbbing heartbeat of Jesus' movement.' ∎

C Wess Daniels, Evangelical pastor, US

C Wess Daniels, correspondence with the author, 3 September 2009.

---

**Freedoms in conflict**

The cause of religious liberty is hampered by religious leaders and activists who promote liberty for themselves while denying it to others. When a religion holds the allegiance of the majority of a country's population, it is not uncommon to hear a number of its adherents argue that it should be granted privileged status. Right-wing Indians speak of 'hindutva', the supposed spirit of Hinduism, seen as the heritage of the Indian subcontinent. This idea was developed by the nationalist VD Savarkar (1883-1966), who effectively graded faith communities, with religions such as Buddhism and Sikhism regarded as within the spirit of hindutva, but Islam and Christianity labeled as 'foreign'. In Britain, the conservative Church of England priest David Holloway argues that 'it is not unreasonable – indeed, it is wise – for the Christian faith and not other faiths to be privileged'.[9]

These attitudes can occur not only when one religious group claims privileges denied to the rest but when a law seeks to protect religion generally. In 2009, a newspaper editor in India was arrested and charged with 'deliberately acting with malicious intent to outrage religious feelings'[10] after he published an article by the New Atheist writer Johann Hari. Physical violence had erupted outside the offices of the publication that printed it. The intention of such laws appears to be the prevention of religious conflict, but by denying freedom of speech, they often serve to fuel conflict between those with religious and non-religious worldviews.

Thankfully, within any religion whose leaders seek to deny freedom to others, there are usually those who insist that they should be standing up for religious equality. Following the overthrow of apartheid in South Africa in 1994, the Call of Islam, a left-wing Muslim group, expressed outrage at those Muslims who used their newfound freedom to campaign for restrictions on other people's liberty:

> *They hid in the shadow... while the army and their third force generals were killing in the townships. Why did the guardians of morality wait for better days before speaking up? Did they not always believe in the morality of Islam or was the Qur'an silent before 1994? The Prophet said that the greatest jihad is to speak the truth in the face of a tyrant. Why did they wait for others to kill the tyrant and then use the freedom of speech that others fought for to speak?... Now we must ask ourselves whether insincere people should be allowed to fly the flag of Islam on our behalf?*[11]

Another example occurred in 2007, when the British Parliament brought in legislation prohibiting discrimination against same-sex couples in the provision of goods and services. Conservative Christian groups claimed that this was an abuse of religious liberty as it denied them their right to act on their belief that same-sex partnerships are sinful. The inconsistency of their claim was illustrated by the liberal Church of England priest Giles Fraser, who pointed out that Christians 'believe gluttony is a sin, but they haven't been campaigning for Christian waiters to have the right to refuse fat people extra chips'.[12]

To understand what this dispute was really about, it is helpful to note that the religious groups protesting were mostly those who expressed worry about Britain losing its 'Christian heritage' and who had latched on to opposition to homosexuality as a cause around which they could unite. The complaints were not primarily coming from smaller or more marginalized groups sidelined by the political process. They were an example of a relatively influential group feeling under threat as its status declined.

There is a similar picture in many countries in which members of the dominant religion seek to defend their position in societies becoming more religiously diverse. This is perhaps most visible in post-Christendom, the situation prevailing in those societies in which Christianity has traditionally been linked to state power but which are now seeing a greater plurality of religions and worldviews. Christians tend to cling on to their remaining privileges while other religions jostle for space and secularists seek to reduce the influence of them all. In Canada, the Christian Heritage Party argues that government actions should never contravene what it describes as 'biblical ethics', with which of course it identifies its own policies.[13] Talk of 'Christian heritage' usually ignores the reality that in many Christian-majority countries, non-Christian religions have existed for much longer than is often acknowledged. Australia, for example, almost certainly had contact with Islam earlier than it encountered Christianity, due to the visits of Indonesian Muslim fisherpeople and traders to the north of the island long before it was 'discovered' by Europeans.

Those who seek to preserve the status of a dominant religion often miss the point that a majority religion is likely, simply by virtue of numbers, to carry more influence than other religions, even if they are held to be equal in law. Groups and individuals who campaign for privileges for religions that are already in the majority are more often motivated by fear of a loss of standing rather than any serious threat to their liberty.

Dominant religious groups which find themselves in this position do not necessarily oppose all freedom for other groups, but are often against granting them the same level of freedom that they enjoy themselves. Some such groups declare their belief in 'tolerance' of other religions, a word also used by a number of secularists to describe their approach to religion generally. The word 'tolerance' has rather negative associations, implying a willingness to accept something in spite of disapproval. To tolerate something is effectively to 'put up' with it.

Support for religious liberty, on the other hand, means rejecting the notion that religion is about a competition for superior status. This is not to suggest that there is any approach to the issue that can easily solve the complex questions of competing freedoms and religious conflict in society and politics. However, a positive understanding of religious liberty in the context of human rights is likely to offer more effectiveness and equality than negative tolerance. Such a model recognizes that people of many religions and worldviews can play a positive part in an inclusive and democratic society. As Stuart Murray writes:

> *Religious liberty treats convictions seriously, accepts faith communities hold divergent views, respects their freedom to make competing*

> *truth claims, encourages exchanges of views,*
> *identifies secularism as another faith position,*
> *rejects inducement and coercion and develops*
> *ways to protect minorities from oppression.*
> *It invites members of a plural society to*
> *be equally passionate about defending the*
> *freedom of others to hold religious views*
> *they disagree with as about sharing their own*
> *convictions.*[14]

Such a confident vision of religious liberty welcomes
plurality with honesty and enthusiasm rather than
approaching it with reluctance or denial. Most
countries, and most religious groups, have a long way
to go to embrace such a vision.

**1** Brenda E Brasher, *Give Me That Online Religion* (Rutgers University Press, 2004). **2** Kate Loewenthal, *Religion and Mental Health* (Chapman and Hall, 1995). **3** Lucy Bushill-Matthews, *Welcome to Islam: A convert's tale* (Continuum, 2008). **4** Kate Zebiri, *British Muslim Converts: Choosing alternative lives* (Oneworld Publications, 2008). **5** Huw Spanner, 'Rushing to save the world' (interview with Tamsin Omond) in *Third Way*, May 2009. **6** Karen Armstrong, *The Great Transformation* (Atlantic Books, 2006). **7** Cited by Adam Hochschild, *Bury the Chains* (Pan Books, 2006). **8** Kristine Rodstol, 'Headscarves, religion and the state: the reality of European commitment to human rights for all', *Forum 18 News*, 17 March 2004. **9** David Holloway, *Church and State in the New Millennium* (Harper Collins, 2000). **10** Johann Hari, 'Despite the riots and threats, I stand by what I wrote', *Independent*, 12 February 2009. **11** Cited by Farid Esack, *Qur'an, Liberation and Pluralism* (Oneworld Publications, 1997). **12** Giles Fraser, 'Christians must stand against discrimination', *Ekklesia*, 15 January 2007. **13** Christian Heritage Party of Canada website, http://www.chp.ca/en/policy/principles.html, accessed 5 September 2009. **14** Stuart Murray, *Post-Christendom* (Paternoster Press, 2004).

# 7 Sacred violence, sacred peace

**Many of the world's most effective campaigns for peace, as well as remarkable examples of nonviolent resistance, have been motivated by religious commitment. Yet these traditions can easily be overlooked, swamped by the seemingly never-ending news of religious violence and the constant linking of religion with acts of war or terrorism.**

IT WOULD BE unfair and unrepresentative to look at one side of religion's relationship with peace and violence without considering the other. Most religious approaches to these issues can be grouped, very roughly, into three categories. First, traditions of religious pacifism and sacred nonviolence suggest that abstaining from violence carries divine blessing and is the best or only ethical option. Second, notions of holy war are based on the conviction that violence is blessed if carried out against enemies of the divine and that to engage in such violence is both a duty and an honor. Third, a range of compromises between these two positions regard violence as regrettable but sometimes necessary and so seek to lay down criteria for when it is acceptable.

### Religious pacifism

An appreciation of the sanctity of nonviolence can be found at least 3,000 years ago in the Indian subcontinent. There we find the vital concept of '*ahimsa*' – of which 'nonviolence' is effectively a translation. *Ahimsa* can also be translated as 'non-injury' to any person and often to any animal or even to the environment. The most extreme commitment to *ahimsa* is found in Jainism, as we can see from the *Acaranga Sutra*, a Jain scripture deriving from around the fourth century BCE:

> *All breathing, existing, living, sentient creatures should not be slain, nor treated with*

*violence, nor abused, nor tormented, nor
driven away. This is the pure, unchangeable,
eternal law... We corrupt ourselves as soon as
we intend to corrupt others. We kill ourselves
as soon as we intend to kill others... Knowing
this, a wise person should not cause any pain
to any creatures.*[1]

Few would go so far as the Jain monks who
sweep insects from their path to avoid treading on
them. However, many strands of Hinduism have
also given a central place to nonviolence. Gandhi
described the doctrine of *ahimsa* as 'the chief glory
of Hinduism'.[2] The Buddhists' 'middle path' means
they reject Jain asceticism, but they often display a
strong commitment to peace and in many parts of
the world they are known for both their pacifism and
their vegetarianism. The nonviolence of several South
Asian religious traditions is to some extent related
to their belief in reincarnation. For example, respect
for animal life is encouraged by the notion that an
animal's soul may soon be a human's soul, or may
have been such in the past.

Around the same time that Jainism was taking form
in India, the Chinese thinker Mozi (c. 468-371 BCE) –
who initially followed Confucianism but later turned
away from it – urged love for all people and called
for a rejection of war. His book *Against Offensive
Warfare* may be the oldest systematic argument for
nonviolence at a political level. He insisted that the
killing of hundreds of people – as happened in war –
was logically many times worse than a single murder.
He also analyzed the economic effects of warfare to
point out that wars rarely bring long-term benefits to
the states that wage them.

Traditions of nonviolence can also be found in the
Abrahamic religions, although often in a marginal
way. As we have seen, Christianity was predominantly

pacifist until its co-option by the Roman Empire in the fourth century. Since then, there have always been Christian groups who have rejected violence, often attracting persecution from the Christian establishment. Some of these have been monastic groups who have seen this commitment as only for the few. Others, such as Waldensians, Mennonites and Quakers, have argued that nonviolence is an essential aspect of following Christ.

While religions such as Islam and Judaism contain few absolute pacifists, there have still been those who have sought to follow these faiths in firmly nonviolent ways. The Ahmaddiya branch of Islam, founded in the 19th century, emphasizes nonviolence, as have several Sufi traditions. A number of Jewish movements have promoted nonviolence during the last century.

Unfortunately, religious commitment to nonviolence is rarely as well publicized as religious violence. The Maori theologian Donald S Tamihere argues that the frequent Maori refusal to react violently against European colonizers was due to a spiritual and ethical opposition to violence, although the colonizers

---

### Thou shalt not kill

Leonard Seversky was a soldier in the US army before becoming a pacifist in 1990. In his application for Conscientious Objector status, he set out the reasons for his change of heart:

'I am without a doubt unable, due to ethical, moral and religious convictions, to participate in any organization whose primary purpose is to wage war and end human life. The reason that I am seeking separation from the Armed Forces is primarily due to the maturing of my ethical, moral and religious beliefs. I am a Jew and I believe in the Ten Commandments, which includes the Commandment "Thou Shalt Not Kill"... The whole basis of Judaism is to treat your fellow man as you want to be treated. There is nothing that could justify the taking of human life in any situation. War is killing and killing is wrong.' ∎

Leonard Seversky, '"Killing is Wrong": A Jewish CO's story' in *The Challenge of Shalom,* edited by Murray Polner and Naomi Goodman (New Society Publishers, 1994).

triumphantly attributed it to weakness.[3] Similarly, when Native Americans of the Hopi tradition acted on their historic peace commitment by refusing to fight in World War One, they were accused of tribal disloyalty to the United States.

### Holy war

The phrase 'holy war' now often appears in the media in relation to religiously motivated terrorism. The essence of the holy war approach is to see violence not as a regrettable necessity but as both a religious duty and a noble privilege. While the word 'terrorism' is ambiguous, it has much in common with holy war if it is taken to mean a willingness to kill innocent people for the glory of a supposedly greater cause. However, such attitudes have often been demonstrated by supporters of conventional wars as well as by the sort of groups to whom the word 'terrorist' is most commonly applied.

In many religions, traditions of sanctified violence have run parallel with traditions of nonviolence, often existing in tension and sometimes with one or the other gaining the upper hand. Despite the Indian notion of *ahimsa*, the epics and scriptures of Hinduism have been used to call down divine blessing on violence. Shri Nathuramj Godse, who assassinated Gandhi in 1948, quoted the *Bhagavad Gita* in support of his action – the same text which Gandhi himself cited as his greatest inspiration. When a right-wing Hindu mob stormed and destroyed a mosque in Ayodhya in 1992, they claimed to be doing so for the glory of Lord Rama, an incarnation of the God Vishnu, who was believed to have been born on the site. They expressed their outrage that a Muslim place of worship should cover Rama's birthplace, although it had been there since the 16th century.

It is in Christianity that the notion of holy war has been strongest, having developed firmly in the 11th century. In 1096, Pope Urban II called on Christians to wage a 'crusade' against Muslims, Jews, Pagans and 'heretics' (meaning those Christian groups not in union with the Roman Church). The crusades, which continued for several centuries, were portrayed by Church and political leaders as military pilgrimages, earning God's approval for the Christians who fought in them. Notions of holy war have resurfaced in Christianity ever since. After Britain went to war with Germany in 1914, the Bishop of London, Arthur F Winnington-Ingram, labeled it a holy war and told British troops to:

> *Kill Germans. Kill them, not for the sake of killing, but to save the world. Kill the good as well as the bad, kill the young as well as the old, kill those who have shown kindness to our wounded. As I have said a thousand times, I look upon it as a war for purity, I look upon everyone who dies in the war as a martyr.*[4]

Christians wishing to sanctify violence have often drawn selectively on the Hebrew Bible (the Old Testament to Christians). There are certainly passages in it which suggest that God blesses violence, sometimes of the most extreme variety, such as against the children of an enemy. While some would argue that these texts are not representative and emerged in particular historical settings, this has not stopped both Jews and Christians using them in support of far more recent actions.

In Judaism, however, the notion of sacred violence had all but died out until the establishment of the State of Israel in the 20th century. Jewish extremists now proclaim that God gives military blessing to Israel's forces. A soldier involved in the Israeli attack on Gaza in 2009 reported that a rabbi had declared to troops that they were 'conducting the war of the "sons of light" against the "sons of darkness"'.[5]

However, it is with Islam that much of the media today tends to associate the phrase 'holy war'. It is frequently used as a – very inaccurate – translation of the Muslim concept of 'jihad', which in reality translates as 'struggle'. Muhammad taught that there were two jihads. The Greater Jihad is the inner struggle to serve God and confront our lower nature. The Lesser Jihad is the outward struggle for justice and righteousness. The latter may occasionally take the form of armed resistance to oppression, but for most Muslims this is an extreme situation. However, the word is now employed by terrorist leaders such as Osama bin Laden to suggest that God has blessed massacres of innocent civilians. The majority of Muslims, opposing such attacks, struggle to assert that jihad does not mean holy war.

## Just war

The most influential approach to war in most religions (as well as in the secular world) has been one that regards violence as a regrettable necessity that should be severely limited. This view is often referred to as 'just war', a phrase associated with certain Christian thinkers but also used by others. 'Just war' differs from 'holy war' in that it seeks to lay down criteria for when violence is acceptable, rather than assuming that waging war in the name of a religion or a deity is automatically right and glorious.

Several Chinese religious traditions emphasize the restriction of war to limited and extreme situations. The Daoist scripture *Daodejing* asserts that 'the ruler imbued with the Dao will not use the force of arms to subdue other countries'[6] but accepts that not all rulers follow the Dao and that it is therefore right to be prepared to use limited violence in self-defense. However, this is not something to be welcomed, as the *Daodejing* makes clear:

*Arms are instruments of ill omens... One who has the Dao does not abide by their use... When one is compelled to use them, it is best to do so without relish. There is no glory in victory, and to glorify it despite this is to exult in the killing of men. One who exults in the killing of men will never have his way in the empire.*[7]

The Confucian *Analects* quote K'ung Tzu as teaching the three duties of government to be providing food, providing arms and gaining the people's trust. He famously said that arms should be the first to go if the government was faced with difficult choices. In the fourth century BCE, the Confucian teacher Meng Ke, while emphasizing the desirability of peace when possible, stated that violence is acceptable to overthrow a tyrant.

Sikhism also provides a good example of a religion with a strong view of the acceptability of war in certain situations. Its founder, Guru Nanak, focused on reconciliation but believed that war could be justified in extreme circumstances. This was taken further by the 10th Sikh Guru, Gobind Singh (1666-1708), who responded to the oppression of Sikhs by establishing a Sikh army. While he showed a mystical devotion to the army that at times looked similar to a 'holy war' approach, he was keen to emphasize that they fought to resist persecution, 'to uproot evil and protect from tyranny the weak and oppressed'.[8]

Much Hindu thinking suggests that, while nonviolence is the ideal, it is not possible for everyone, and people at different stages of life and spiritual discipline may have to compromise. Buddhists who have excused violence in certain circumstances include the influential scholar Enryo Inoue, who argued in 1905 that Japanese Buddhists could fight in their country's war with Russia because they did so defensively.

## Sacred violence, sacred peace

In Judaism, the Mishnah – which forms the basis of the Talmud – outlines two types of war. The first is a *milhemet mitzvah*, a necessary war, generally fought for self-defense. All but a small minority of pacifist Jews accept that war is acceptable in cases of self-defense, but they differ on the acceptability of the other type of war, a *milhemut reshut*, or optional war.

However, it is perhaps in Christianity that criteria for 'just war' have been worked through most systematically. Following its adoption as the religion of the Roman Empire, Christianity's originally pacifist nature was abandoned and theologians such as Augustine of Hippo (354-430) argued that Jesus' teachings on peace applied only to individuals, not states. Augustine told a soldier that 'peace should be the object of your desire; war should be waged only as a necessity'.[9] He built on the just war theory developed by the Pagan thinker Cicero (106-43 BCE) and laid down criteria in which war could be considered acceptable. These criteria became blurred over time, with Christians quoting various factors for what constituted a just war. More recently, Christian theologians such as Rienhold Niebuhr have arrived at a just war position from slightly different starting-points. Niebuhr argued against both pacifism and holy war on grounds of realism, suggesting that wars must be fought but that they are the result of sin.

Muslim notions of just war began after Muhammad and his followers established a community in Medina to escape persecution in Mecca. He allowed that a defensive war was acceptable when the Pagan authorities attacked his community. However, he insisted that children, women and old men should never be killed, nor should anyone who gave himself up to God, even by a single utterance. Following Muhammad's death, the power of his successors increased and later Muslim leaders fought many more wars against non-Muslim states. Although many maintained that Muslims should fight only in defense and not provoke wars with non-Muslims, there was a tendency to see these conflicts as continuations of the battles of Muhammad, despite his strict criteria.

## Making comparisons

While holy war and pacifism are in many ways direct opposites, they have something in common with each other that they do not share with 'just war' theory. They both seek to start from the point of what is spiritually right – or 'God's will' in many traditions – rather than with the temporary political situation with which they are faced. However, while the rhetoric of holy war tends to provoke shock and outrage, only a relatively small minority of religious justifications for war really fall into this category. Far more wars have been supported by religious groups and their leaders using 'just war' arguments.

These include conflicts in which both sides have claimed that ethics supported their case. This has often involved each side claiming justification on the basis of the same religion. In the war between Argentina and Britain in 1982, several Christian leaders in both countries argued that their government was fighting a just war.

There are clearly widely varying views of what constitutes a just war. One commentator, observing the influence of 'just war' theory on the secular world suggests: 'It is dominant without being clear. It has taken over without being tested.'[10] The Christian pacifist Walter Wink says, somewhat scathingly: 'Most Christians assume that any war they *feel* is just, or merely necessary and unavoidable, *is* just'.[11] The Sri Lankan Buddhist monk Walpola Rahula mocks the whole concept of a just war by suggesting that 'the mighty and the victorious are "just" and the weak and the defeated are "unjust"'.[12]

One reason for this controversy is the flexibility

of the criteria that many religious thinkers have laid down for determining a just war. The most common issue they mention tends to be self-defense. This is of course understandable, but self-defense is a far from straightforward concept. When Al-Qaeda killed thousands with their attacks on New York and Washington in 2001, several Muslim fundamentalists described it as an act of self-defense. Two years later, the US and British governments justified their invasion of Iraq by claiming that the Iraqi regime was a threat to its people, whom they were acting to defend. Some would say that self-defense includes going to the aid of someone else who is being attacked, but states typically only go to war to defend another state if it is an established ally or if they have a political or commercial interest in doing so.

This tendency to adapt the principle to fit the war, rather than the other way round, is common amongst many of those who speak of just war. The Muslim writer Rabia Terri Harris points out how certain Muslim theorists defend violence by comparing the Muslim communities of today's world with Muhammad's community when it was under attack:

> The current community lacks much of a resemblance to the community of the Prophet. But... these theorists undertake strenuous efforts to make it fit. Among activists, this may mean pressurizing present-day Muslims to more closely approximate [to] the image of those Muslims who were liberated long ago – thus producing real oppression for the sake of an imagined liberation. Or it may mean redefining 'the enemy' to signify something the Prophet never would have allowed.[13]

Nonetheless, some supporters of 'just war' theory argue that, while the term has been abused to justify all manner of violence, it is still meaningful if based on very strict criteria. Certain Christians suggest that Augustine's originally rigid requirements have been modified, watered down and deliberately twisted over time. Different versions and variations of these criteria exist, but they generally include principles that war must be fought for a just cause, be declared by a legitimate authority, have a peaceful intention, be fought with proportionality, have a reasonable chance of success and be undertaken only as a last resort.

It is not difficult to see how these requirements can be manipulated. They are open to widely varying interpretations, even by those genuinely seeking to apply them. However, the strictest interpretations would rule out most wars that have ever been fought. Some argue that they rule out all wars in our own time, particularly if the criterion of proportionality is taken to bar attacks on civilians – who now account for over 90 per cent of all war casualties. This provides a contrast to just war theorists such as Niebuhr, who was prepared to countenance the use of nuclear weapons, albeit only in the most extreme circumstances.

It appears that the criteria, while vague, could be useful if those who speak of just war were all taking them seriously. The main problem is not the vagueness of the criteria – though that doesn't help – but rather that most religious leaders tend to support wars in which they find their country happens to be involved, and to support their own government's role in it. As we have seen, most religious leaders are reluctant to challenge the powerful. Their default position of accepting the status quo means accepting the wars that come with it.

### A real alternative

However, not everyone who dismisses nonviolence and pacifism is simply repelled by their radicalism. Others have been put off by what they regard as pacifists' tendency to be unrealistic or to withdraw from the world. This may be a caricature of pacifism but it is not without foundation. For some religious groups, such as Jehovah's Witnesses, the refusal to engage in warfare is part of their wider refusal to participate in politics or take part in social or economic disputes. Other groups have been pushed into a position of withdrawal by their experience of persecution.

Many pacifists have demonstrated little interest in putting forward alternative proposals for approaching world problems, often seeming to be more concerned with their own purity. These attitudes have frustrated and angered other pacifists as much as anyone else. As Walter Wink puts it:

> *Some pacifists have been rightly criticized for being more concerned with their own righteousness than with the sufferings of the afflicted... The issue is not, "What must I do in order to secure my salvation?" but rather, "What does God require of me in response to the needs of others?"... Otherwise our nonviolence is premised on self-justifying attempts to establish our own purity in the eyes of God, others and ourselves, and that is nothing less than a satanic temptation to die with clean hands and a dirty heart.*[14]

Pacifists such as Wink emphasize that nonviolence is about changing the world rather than withdrawing from it. They suggest it involves belief that there is always an alternative to war and that humanity is not inherently violent. As such, it is not about neutrality or passivity – it is not 'passivism'. Such pacifists argue that choosing pacifism means rejecting the dominant values of the world and that this means engaging in nonviolent conflict. They draw a clear distinction between *conflict*, which occurs when people have incompatible goals, and *violence*, which involves inflicting physical or emotional harm in response to conflict.

Such an approach attracts support from many who do not consider themselves to be pacifists but who recognize the power of nonviolence. Some of these choose the latter term rather than the former because they hold that there are a tiny number of situations in which violence is the right response. This approach has been notable amongst certain Muslim writers such as Rabia Terri Harris and Bawa Muhaiyaddeen, but attracts support from many others. Some have sought to develop entirely new terms to avoid negative associations. Gandhi created the word 'satyagraha', derived from words that mean 'soul force' or 'truth force'. The Christian theologian Noel Moules coined the term 'shalom activism', based on the biblical word 'shalom', which is often translated as 'peace', but also includes justice, wholeness and the restoration of healthy and equal relationships.

The phrase 'active nonviolence' is sometimes used as an umbrella term for these approaches. Walter Wink suggests that nonviolence is an approach that allows pacifists who believe in meaningful engagement to find common cause with the minority of 'just war' theorists who are prepared to apply their criteria in a very strict way to impose severe limitations on violence.

Gandhi argued that nonviolence was not a middle way between passivity and violent resistance. Rather, it was *more* radical than a violent response, because it sought to resist the violence of oppression without using violence in return. Theologians in many religions, as well as secular thinkers, have drawn on Gandhi's insights. He was very keen that nonviolence should be a practical and realistic approach, offering 'a moral equivalent to war'. This required the 'stoutest hearts' willing to accept their own suffering and even death in effective nonviolent resistance rather than resorting to violence against others.[15]

While much talk of nonviolence has focused on resistance to oppression, others have drawn on aspects of their religious traditions to develop methods of nonviolent conflict resolution. The Jewish theologian Dan Cohn-Sherbok suggests that Jews 'have an important lesson to teach the world's peacemakers' because of the skills and practices they have developed that have taught them how 'to express, how to accept and how to deal with difference amongst themselves'.[16] The US Buddhist Christopher S Queen points out that:

> *The Buddhist tradition is often praised for its peace teachings... While these praises are justified, it is important to recognize that Buddhism's contribution lies not primarily in its commitment to peace per se – most world religions are committed to 'peace' in some fashion – but in the unique perspectives and techniques Buddhists have developed for achieving peace within and between individuals and groups.*[17]

There are now a number of international organizations focused on nonviolent approaches to conflict. For example, Responding to Conflict (RTC) is an international NGO that offers training and support to people in areas of conflict to help them build peace in their own communities. Although RTC is not based on any one faith, other projects have a specifically religious basis, such as Christian Peacemaker Teams and the Ecumenical Accompaniment Programme in Palestine and Israel (EAPPI). Both of these provide people to work in areas of conflict monitoring and promoting peace and human rights.

But we are still left with the question: What has this to do with religion? It may be a positive thing for people to promote nonviolence, but does their religion have anything to do with it, or is it merely incidental?

### Transforming power

Many people choose to commit themselves to nonviolence without being affected by the element of religion. Some even reject both violence and religion on the same grounds. The atheist pacifist Albert Beale sees religion as irrational and hence as a form of 'mental dehumanization'. He argues that it is the same dehumanizing attitude that 'leads to people's willingness to kill one another; hence rejection of religion and rejection of violence are inseparable'.[18]

Nonetheless, Beale willingly works alongside many religious individuals in his peace activism. Some argue that it is this practical action that matters, rather than the motivations. While there is some validity to this point, it can lead us to say that nonviolent religious activists would have worked for peace anyway, with

---

### The rulers of the world?

'To kill one man is to be guilty of a capital crime, to kill ten men is to increase the guilt ten-fold, to kill a hundred men is to increase it a hundred-fold. This the rulers of the earth all recognize and yet when it comes to the greatest crime – waging war on another state – they praise it!...

'If a man on seeing a little black were to say it is black, but on seeing a lot of black were to say it is white, it would be clear that such a man could not distinguish black and white. Or if he were to taste a few bitter things [but] were to pronounce them sweet, clearly he would be incapable of distinguishing between sweetness and bitterness. So those who recognize a small crime as such, but do not recognize the wickedness of the greatest crime of all – the waging of war on another state – but actually praise it, cannot distinguish right and wrong. So as to right and wrong, the rulers of the world are in confusion.' ∎
Mozi, fifth century BCE

Cited by Mark Kurlansky, *Nonviolence: The history of a dangerous idea* (Jonathan Cape, 2006).

or without their religion. This is probably true in some cases, but many people have been moved to nonviolence by a re-examination of their own religion. Take Abdul Ghaffar Khan (1890-1988), who was imprisoned for working against British rule in India. Reading the Qur'an in jail, he developed a new appreciation of the patience and dedication of Muhammad. 'I had read it all before, as a child,' he said. 'But now I read it in the light of what I was hearing all around me about Gandhi's struggle'. This led to his commitment to nonviolence, which 'changed my life forever'.[19] He came to be nicknamed 'the frontier Gandhi'.

Just as a re-examination of religious traditions has helped many who seek to take sides against injustice, it has also motivated some to choose nonviolence. This at times involves rejecting well-established but inaccurate perceptions of historical religious teachings. For example, Jesus said 'if anyone strikes you on the right cheek, turn the other also'.[20] Many have seen this as an encouragement to passivity in the face of aggression, but scholars and activists point to the context of the saying. Someone can only be struck on the right cheek by the right hand if the aggressor is using the back of his/her hand. This was not a fistfight; it was the way in which people humiliated supposed social inferiors. Wives were backhanded by their husbands, slaves by their masters and Jewish civilians by Roman soldiers. Jesus advocated neither violent resistance nor cowering submission but an assertion of dignity. Turning the other cheek signals to the aggressor that he/she has failed in the attempt to humiliate and that the intended victim asserts his/her equality.

This is but one example of the way in which traditional religious teachings, when detached from centuries of accommodation with forces of power and war, provide encouragement for nonviolent engagement. However, as with the examples of political resistance that we have looked at, there is another important factor involved. Deep religious commitment provides a different base from which to approach the world, rather than the coincidences of political convenience and compromise. A spiritual starting-point suggests the possibility of taking a step back from the concerns of the moment and looking at basic principles. As we have seen in the case of holy war, such a starting-point can lead to unbridled brutality and terror. Alternatively, a recognition of powers beyond the transient authorities of the world moves people to confidence that the violence and oppression that they find around them do not represent the ultimate reality of existence. They can be defeated.

This understanding of the link between spirituality, power and activism can be found in a large number of religious traditions of nonviolence. It explains why mystically inclined movements such as Sufism and Quakerism are so often those that actively reject violence. Gandhi said that 'whilst everything around me is changing, everything dying, there is underlying all that change a living power that is changeless, that holds all together'.[21] The Cheyenne peace chief Lawrence Hart suggests that it is an awareness of spiritual power that allows Native American groups to make decisions peacefully and to remain united.[22] In the Sufi tradition, such awareness involves recognizing the 'real' nature of everything we come across, rather than the apparent realities of personal interest and convenience. The peace activist Helen Steven describes the experience which transformed her understanding of power and infused her nonviolent activism:

> *For a few moments I had experienced a power and outrage beyond myself, and this showed that that special power which Jesus had is also available to me. This is the power that inspired the prophets, Gandhi, Martin Luther King,*

## Sacred violence, sacred peace

*Rosa Parks, Dorothy Day – and me. It was an extraordinarily exciting discovery... It was precisely this very question of authority and source of power that constituted the offense of Jesus to the religious leaders of his time... So now it came to me with blinding clarity that claiming this power and letting it drive where it must, leads straight into trouble.*[23]

The link between spiritual commitment and nonviolent activism has been drawn by many people, but they have usually been on the margins of religions. A key challenge for religious groups in the 21st century is to make this link apparent. This involves more than rejecting holy war. It means actively opposing situations in which religious groups become mouthpieces for governments wishing to wage war for their own ends. Such an approach requires a religious shift of global proportions.

**1** Cited by Christopher Key Chapple, 'Jainism and Nonviolence' in *Subverting Hatred: The challenge of nonviolence in religious traditions*, edited by Daniel L Smith-Christopher (Orbis Books, 2007). **2** Mohandas Gandhi, 'A Talk' [1946] in *Soul Force: Gandhi's writings on peace*, edited by V Geetha (Tara Publishing, 2004). **3** Donald S Tamihere, 'The Struggle for Peace: Subverting hatred in a Maori context' in *Subverting Hatred*, op cit. **4** Cited by Ian Hazlett, 'War and Peace in Christianity' in *War and Peace in World Religions*, edited by Perry Schmidt-Leukel (SCM Press, 2004). **5** *Operation Cast Lead* (Breaking the Silence, 2009). **6** Cited by Mark Kurlansky, *Nonviolence: The history of a dangerous idea* (Jonathan Cape, 2006). **7** Cited by Tam Wai Lun, 'Subverting Hatred' in *Subverting Hatred* op cit. **8** Cited by Oliver McTernan, *Violence in God's Name* (Darton, Longman and Todd, 2003). **9** Cited by Oliver McTernan, op cit. **10** John Howard Yoder, *The Priestly Kingdom: Social ethics as Gospel* (University of Notre Dame Press, 1984). **11** Walter Wink, *Engaging the Powers: Discernment and resistance in a world of domination* (Fortress Press, 1992). **12** Walpola Rahula, 'The Social Teachings of the Buddha' in *The Path of Compassion*, edited by Fred Eppsteiner (Parallax Press, 1988). **13** Rabia Terri Harris, 'Nonviolence in Islam' in *Subverting Hatred* op cit. **14** Walter Wink, *Jesus and Nonviolence* (Fortress Press, 2003). **15** Terrence J Rynne, *Gandhi and Jesus: The saving power of nonviolence* (Orbis Books, 2008). **16** Dan Cohn-Sherbok, 'War and Peace in Judaism' in *War and Peace in World Religions*, op cit. **17** Christopher S Queen, 'The Peace Wheel' in *Subverting Hatred* op cit. **18** Albert Beale, correspondence with the author, 21 August 2009. **19** Cited by Shireen Shah, *The Frontier Gandhi: Abdul Ghaffar Khan, Muslim champion of nonviolence* (Movement for the Abolition of War, 2008). **20** Matthew 5, 39, *The*

*Bible, New Revised Standard Version* (Cambridge University Press, 1993). **21** Cited by Terrence J Rynne, op cit.. **22** Daniel L Smith-Christopher, 'Indigenous Traditions of Peace: An interview with Lawrence Hart, Cheyenne peace chief' in *Subverting Hatred* op cit. **23** Helen Steven, *No Extraordinary Power* (Quaker Books, 2005).

# 8 The future

**Religion began over 30,000 years ago. Only in the last two centuries have there been predictions that it will one day end. But as long as people have the need to search for meaning beyond themselves, religion will be a central feature of human life.**

SCHOLARS IN THE early 20th century who forecast the imminent end of religion have turned out to be mistaken. Predictions of religion's demise resurfaced in the 1960s and 1970s, due to the decline of institutional Christianity in certain Western countries and the tendency of Western scholars not to look at what was going on in the rest of the globe. Even those parts of the world that have seen significant religious change show no sign of witnessing the end of religion as a whole, but rather the replacement of certain forms of religion and spirituality with others.

Nonetheless, the forms that religion takes are constantly changing and difficult to predict. No-one can be confident of what will happen to religion in the next 10 years, let alone the next 100 or the next 1,000. However, looking around the world, it is possible to make tentative predictions about the challenges that religious groups and movements are likely to face in the immediate future.

First, the ongoing globalization of communication will change religion in ways that we can only begin to imagine. It is already threatening religious authority, allowing a greater sharing of grassroots religious thought and exposing people to ideas about religion that they would not otherwise encounter. This is likely to increase the fluidity of religious boundaries, meaning more people will be influenced by a variety of religious movements and make their commitments accordingly. Some religious groups and their leaders will continue to fight against the openness that the internet brings, while others are likely to ignore its impact and pretend that nothing has changed. In contrast, those religious movements that welcome these developments as exciting opportunities are likely to function most effectively and attract the most interest.

Second, religious groups are likely to find themselves caught up in even more conflicts over power, status and liberty as more and more societies become religiously diverse. The movement of people, ideas, organizations and businesses means that fewer and fewer societies will be dominated by a single religion. Some dominant religious groups will clearly continue to react to this sort of situation with fierce defensiveness, some happy for tyrants to suppress religious liberty while others plead implausibly that their privileged status is compatible with democracy. Religious groups that are gaining influence may be tempted by a desire to replace dominant religions rather than to exist alongside them. The religions that will thrive best in plural societies are those that embrace religious equality, seeking co-operation where they agree and respectful dialogue where they do not, confident enough of their position not to rely on privilege or prejudice.

Third, religions will face challenges over their priorities and purposes. Such challenges are closely tied to their associations with power. Religious groups that continue to ally themselves with oppressive and discriminatory power are unlikely to give any serious attention to the staggering global problems of poverty, inequality, war and environmental destruction. Those that pay more attention to the compassion and love taught by the vast majority of religious founders will put human and environmental wellbeing – often casually dismissed as 'politics' – ahead of struggles for status. This is vital at a time when climate chaos threatens the globe. It is now well established that the poorest people in the poorest countries are likely to be the foremost victims of climate change, but if the worse predictions are fulfilled, few if any will be unaffected by it. Future historians may look back and ask which religious groups occupied this crucial time with compassionate and spiritually motivated attempts to tackle climate chaos and the related problems of poverty and war. It is those movements, not the religious leaders and lobbyists concerned mainly for their own power and prestige, which will earn the respect of future generations.

For almost as long as religion has existed, there have been those who have used it to shore up injustice and those whom it has motivated to struggle for better communities, better lifestyles and a better world. The international spread of ideas and movements is a blessing for those who reject religion's links with oppression and war in favor of a higher loyalty that calls for compassion and justice in religious approaches to politics and people. The bridge between religion and progressive politics is a broad one. It has always existed, and millions have walked freely across it. The gates to the bridge remain open – in both directions.

# Bibliography

Karen Armstrong, *A History of God*, Vintage Books, 1993.

Karen Armstrong, *The Case for God: What religion really means*, The Bodley Head, 2009.

John Bowker (ed), *Oxford Dictionary of World Religions*, Oxford University Press, 1999.

James Cox, *Expressing the Sacred*, University of Zimbabwe Publications, 2000.

Richard Dawkins, *The God Delusion*, Black Swan, 2006.

Thomas Dixon, *Science and Religion*, Oxford University Press, 2008.

Terry Eagleton, *Reason, Faith and Revolution: Reflections on the God debate*, Yale University Press, 2009.

Martin Forward, *Religion: A Beginner's Guide*, Oneworld Publications, 2001.

Marc Gellman and Thomas Hartman, *Religion for Dummies*, John Wiley & Sons, 2002.

Oliver McTernan, *Violence in God's Name*, Darton, Longman and Todd, 2003.

Malory Nye, *Religion: The Basics*, Routledge, 2008.

Christopher Partridge (ed), *Encyclopedia of New Religions*, Lion Publishing, 2004.

*The New Penguin Handbook of Living Religions*, Penguin, 2005.

Ninian Smart, *The World's Religions*, Cambridge University Press, 1998.

Daniel L Smith-Christopher (ed), *Subverting Hatred: The challenge of nonviolence in religious traditions*, Orbis Books, 2007.

# Index

# Index